The Word Gatherer

John L. Heatwole

The Word Gatherer

Oral History Interview
by
Carol Maureen DeHart

Published by Lot's Wife Publishing
Staunton, Virginia
October 2007

Front cover photograph (also on page 3) by Ron Blunt of John Heatwole's carving, "The Word Gatherer," done for the Museum of the Shenandoah Valley in Winchester, Virginia. Photo courtesy of the museum.

Front cover photograph by Bruce Rossenwasser of John L. Heatwole painting his carving of a wooden drum in his Bridgewater, Virginia, workshop. Back cover photograph of John's drum and box also by Bruce Rossenwasser, 1996.

Photographs by John L. Heatwole, courtesy of Miriam Heatwole, unless otherwise noted. All James Madison University photos courtesy of Heatwole #2075, Special Collections, James Madison University Library, Harrisonburg, Virginia 22807. Photo on page 108 by Pat Turner Ritchie.

Pen and ink drawings of the "The Word Gatherer" carving and the map of John Heatwole's travels were done by Jonathan Gehman of Red Barn Studio.

Cover design by Jennifer Wood Monroe of Wood & Associates.
Interior layout by Nancy Sorrells.

Inquiries may be addressed to:
C.M. DeHart
10647 Hollow Rd.
Fulks Run, VA 22830
540-896-6156
cmaureen@earthlink.net

Lot's Wife Publishing
P.O. Box 1844
Staunton, VA 24402
www.lotswifepublishing.com

Library of Congress Control Number: 2007935770
ISBN-13   9781934368022

In Memory of John L. Heatwole
3/24/48 – 11/22/06

Dedicated
to
Miriam Heatwole,
David Heatwole and Stephanie Price

John with son David

THE TRAVELS of JOHN HEATWOLE...

Jon Gehman 07

WEST VIRGINIA

HARDY
FREDERICK
SHENANDOAH
PENDLETON
PAGE
ROCKINGHAM
POCAHONTAS
AUGUSTA
GREENBRIER
HIGHLAND

VIRGINIA

Table of Contents

The Bee

The symbol of the bee buzzed in and out of John's life on many occasions. The bee is in the Heatwole family crest and for that reason John chose to incorporate it onto his workshop sign in Bridgewater, Virginia. The bee, hard at work gathering nectar, was symbolic of John's passion about oral history and gathering folk traditions that would otherwise have been lost.

One of his favorite stories involved the news bees and their power. In 2005 John's description of these insects was published in the Augusta County Historical Society *Bulletin*.

"In many areas of the uplands of Virginia and West Virginia there was once a belief in the power of news bees. News bees are any little bees that sometimes hover in the air right in front of your face. Most people bat them away with the wave of a hand without realizing the power that the little insects were once thought to possess.

People believed that if you asked simple *yes* or *no* questions the news bee would answer in a fashion. If you asked a question like, 'Is my love true to me?' and the answer was 'yes,' the news bee would move up and down a few times. If the answer was 'no,' the insect would fly in a tight horizontal circle. Several uncanny stories about the truth of news bees' answers have been handed down to the present, but they are too involved to share at this time, and they have no humor in them.

However, once a man visited his father-in-law in Franklin in Pendleton County, West Virginia. They were sitting on the porch quietly enjoying an afternoon while looking out over the South Branch River. The son-in-law looked over toward the older man and noticed a small insect hovering before his face. The father-in-law quickly brought his two hands together killing the bug. The son-in-law asked what it had been. His father-in-law answered calmly, 'It was a news bee.' The astonished younger in-law asked incredulously, 'Why did you kill it?' Without hesitation the answer came: 'No news, is good news.'"

Nancy Sorrells
October, 2007

Preface

"And the stories, I just fell in love with those stories."[1]
John Lawrence Heatwole

The finest storyteller I ever knew was my great-uncle, Paul V. Heatwole (1892-1981), who came full force into my life when I was a young adult in search of an identity. Uncle Paul's fortune was his ability to remember and relate in a wonderful fashion tales of a bygone era; his gift was in never closing himself off from anyone who needed a friend.

His presence and his stories let me know who I was and let me understand why, from my earliest recollections, I had harbored twin compulsions—to create things with my hands and to lose myself in tales that took me out of the sphere of day-to-day existence. Uncle Paul introduced me to the potters, blacksmiths, silversmiths, long rifle makers, weavers and loom makers who had been my ancestors and filled my imagination with the rich stories of people who drank deep from the well of life and were moved to do memorable things.

Uncle Paul was nearly blind when I met him, yet he drew me into the stories—I *heard* the machinery of the mill grinding in the background as he described an old man having a barrel of flour hoisted onto his shoulder, and I *saw* the keen look in the sparkling, dark eyes of a gypsy queen as she told a fortune.

He died on February 26, 1981. We hadn't been sure for days whether or not he was aware of anyone's presence, but when I visited him that evening and told him how powerfully he had affected my life and how much I loved him, he squeezed my hand. He died a few minutes after I left. I was relieved that his suffering was over, but still I was crushed by the loss.

That night I dreamed I was wandering through a dark, storm-ravaged forest. The trees were bare of leaves, and they swayed wildly under rolling black and pewter clouds. The trek seemed endless, and the feeling of oppression was almost unbearable.

Finally, I came to the edge of a two-acre clearing. All was tranquil, the sun was shining, and the elements were calm. A small, white, one-room cottage sat in the middle of the grass-carpeted glade. I entered and saw Uncle Paul sitting on a white couch in front of a large window in the back wall. He smiled, patted the cushion beside him and said, "I've been waiting for you. I have a story to tell you."

At that moment I awakened and felt a tremendous burden lift from my heart and mind. Uncle Paul had let me know that he was still by my side. I hope I am an extension of him.

John L. Heatwole
Originally published as the afterword
in *Shenandoah Voices*, 1995.

Burke's Garden in Southwest Virginia

The Bluegrass Valley, Highland County

Courtesy of Allen Litten, Dec. 2005

John Heatwole's friend, Two-Gun Terry

John L. Heatwole
1948 - 2006

"John is a model for what a teacher should be," his wife Miriam said. "His enthusiasm for his subjects grabs the attention of people who aren't usually interested in that sort of thing."[2]

John L. Heatwole had a great love of Virginia's Shenandoah Valley, often wistfully remarking that he would have preferred to have been born there. Well known for his work preserving, collecting, and disseminating the Civil War history and folklore of the Virginias, John interviewed hundreds of people and would ask, "Did you grow up here? Ever hear any witch stories?" And he would ask about superstitions, farming, games, foods, tools or family lore. And then, having an amazing recall for the stories that people told him, he would retell these stories to captivated audiences, weaving a spell with his words and enthralling radio listeners. "I could do that twenty-four hours a day," he had said. "Go on the folklore comedy circuit. Just stand up in front of people."

Although he is gone, John will also long be remembered for his thirty years of intricate, fantastical woodcarvings, which are in museums, libraries, and private collections throughout the United States, Europe, and the Middle East. In 1991, he became the first Virginia artist to be invited by the United States Senate to mount a solo exhibition of his carvings in the Senate Rotunda.

In July of 2006, at fifty-eight years old, John learned that he had inoperable cancer. He was given less than a year to live and notified his devastated friends and colleagues. "We all have to die," he told his friend, Jo Ellen Bowman. "It's just sooner than I had planned."

On October 31, 2006, John was honored with a reception given by the Massanutten Regional Library and the Shenandoah Valley Folklore Society. People that John had worked with gathered in Bridgewater College's Boitnott Room to say hello and goodbye to this beloved historian, folklorist, storyteller, wood carver, author, and friend. In the background, Two-Gun Terry played fiddle, accompanied by a mandolin and a banjo player. Executive Director of the Shenandoah Valley Battlefields Foundation, Howard Kittell, said of John, "He knits the Valley together."

When Bridgewater College President, Dr. Phillip Stone, spoke from the podium, he spoke for us all: "You can't talk to John about history without feeling that passion he has for history.... A kind, decent, and funny guy, we have loved John as we worked with him and we appreciate so much all he's done for our organizations and our Valley. Especially his efforts to nurture and teach us about the heritage we have here. We are glad to have an opportunity to say it to your face: John, thank you, for all you've meant to us in the Shenandoah Valley of Virginia. For what you've done for us, for our heritage and our history and for succeeding generations, to make certain that we preserve something of our heritage that we think is so wonderful. Thank you."

John and I were working on publishing this transcript of his oral history interview when he died in November of 2006. This is not meant as a biography and may not be chronologically accurate when John spoke of his ancestry or other dates. This is John's oral history.

In all of his work, preserving folklore and Civil War history, in the whimsical, wonderful carvings and in the fabulous and fascinating stories, John sparked inspiration in all those around him.

Carol Maureen DeHart
October, 2007

Courtesy of the Museum
of the Shenandoah Valley

On display in the Museum of the Shenandoah Valley's Decorative Arts Gallery in Winchester, Virginia: "The Word Gatherer - John Heatwole - 2004. Wood (Linden), Polychrome Paint. Collectors widely seek the work of contemporary Valley folk artist, John Heatwole. This carving took sixty hours to complete, and was made for this museum. It depicts a man in walking clothes, notebook at the ready to gather stories about the Valley and its people. The subject is appropriate, for this artist is also a folklorist, historian, and author. He has conducted interviews with people throughout the Valley to tell this region's stories."

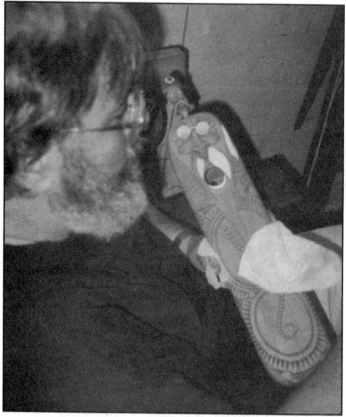

Courtesy of Bruce Rossenwasser

This finger drum is actually two hollowed out pieces of wood, glued together and carved in such a way as to obliterate the seam. The drum is played by tapping on it with the fingers, creating all kinds of different sounds depending on how much or how little of the hole is covered.

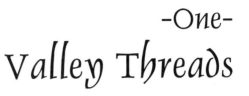

Valley Threads

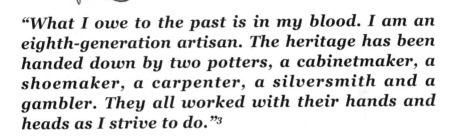

"What I owe to the past is in my blood. I am an eighth-generation artisan. The heritage has been handed down by two potters, a cabinetmaker, a shoemaker, a carpenter, a silversmith and a gambler. They all worked with their hands and heads as I strive to do."[3]

Sunlight, books, and artifacts lined the walls of John L. Heatwole's office in the basement of the Virginia home that he shared with his wife Miriam. A hoodoo doll, corn shuckers, tools, paintings, and file cabinets comfortably filled the room. John and I settled into chairs next to the plate glass doors overlooking their wooded back yard and the upturned apple crate where John scattered squirrel food. John talked about his life and shared favorite stories from the hundreds of interviews he has conducted throughout the Virginias.

Carol DeHart [CD]: It's March 14th.
John Heatwole [JLH]: It's the 15th. (Laughter)

CD: You're right. (Laughter) March 15th, 2004.
JLH: I could put some nuts out for the squirrels. No, you'd have to turn around. Never mind. I put all these split pecans out on that H.F. Byrd apple box and Miriam said, "Six dollars a pound, are you crazy? For split pecans?" I'll be typing away at the computer and they'll be sitting there just eating them. It's a lot of fun.

CD: Great. Your family came to the Valley in the 1700s?

JLH: The Scots-Irish branch came in 1750, here to Augusta County. Then one German branch came to what's now Shenandoah County in 1760. Another German branch came to Rockingham in 1790, so that's how they came in.

All of them came through Pennsylvania, like a lot of the settlers into this area in the eighteenth-century, looking for cheap land and a place, not the religion so much. It was just that the land was very fertile and they could afford it. So they came in in droves.

Except for my great-great-great-great grandfather Heatwole; he came in because he had run away. He was a bond servant to a blacksmith, and the blacksmith beat him, so he came to the Shenandoah Valley looking for his uncle, a Continental soldier, who had been actually an Indian fighter. He had gone on Sullivan's expedition against the Iroquois and things like that. He found him near Turley Town in Rockingham County.

Heatwole went back to Pennsylvania and married a young woman whose family had been pretty much wiped out during the Wyoming massacre during the Revolution and brought her back to the Valley. That's how they came here.

They were here for many, many years and then in the late 1920s, early 1930s, my grandfather took his family to the Washington area. But my father was born here. And I would come down here during the summers when I was a child and spend time.

It was very confusing, I'd spend one summer with Old Order Mennonite relatives and another summer with Church of the Brethren relatives, and another summer with United Brethren relatives. (Laughter) So I wasn't sure what everybody was about because they all seemed to be kind of at odds with each other all the time. But it was really interesting.

CD: When were you born?

JLH: March 24, 1948.

CD: Your birthday's coming right around the corner, what's that, next Wednesday?

JLH: I don't know. (Laughter) This morning at an appointment they asked me how old I was and I had to think about it. I just don't think about things like that. I hardly ever know what day of the week it is.

CD: I've heard you have a lot of artisans in your background.

JLH: Yes. I've never really counted them, but every generation has at least one. And some of the generations have five or six.

Often as not, John was following the ghosts from his own family's past when he tracked down stories like the one described on this history highway marker from Greenbrier, West Virginia, where his ancestors had lived.

Potters, silversmiths. No actual wood carvers. There have been furniture makers. In fact, I have a couple pieces that my grandfather made that are real nice.

The potters are probably the most well known. Andrew Coffman, who is the first documented potter in Rockingham County. And then his daughter married my great-great-grandfather, "Potter" John Heatwole. And he trained Emmanuel Suter, who was his cousin, to throw pots.

Conestoga Connections: The Coffman Conestoga Wagon is on display at the North House Museum in Lewisburg, W.Va.

The first Kauffman who came into Shenandoah County in 1760 was a trouser maker, Christian Kauffman. That's one thing that has changed, it probably started to change in the nineteenth century, before that it was the men that were the weavers. Most people don't realize that. He was an eighteenth-century trouser maker.

There have been quite a number. And the funny part about

it is that, since I was a child I've always had this need to be making something with my hands. And didn't know about all of this until much later.

CD: You just had that impulse, that urge. I've always felt that with writing.

JLH: Oh yes, writing's always been a part of it too. There is another writer in the family, and that's Pearl Buck, who was my grandfather's first cousin once removed. She was from West Virginia. One of her grandparents was a Sidenstricker who was part of the Kauffman family. Real convoluted, but it's in there.

The Kauffmans, who settled in Shenandoah County, my fifth great-grandfather, Christian Kauffman, I believe, left Shenandoah County in 1788 in a Conestoga wagon and went to Greenbrier County. And the wagon is still in existence. It's over at the North House Museum in Lewisburg, West Virginia. It's a beautiful wagon.

One of my other great-great grandfathers, Samuel Coffman, used to drive a Conestoga wagon when he was a boy, with an older cousin. They would take feathers and beeswax and produce and all kinds of stuff in that wagon from Greenbrier County to Baltimore. I forget how many weeks they said it took to do it.

Then they'd buy things there and bring it back to Creigh's store in Lewisburg. Eventually when Samuel grew into young manhood, he came to Rockingham County and met my great-great grandmother and married her and then became the Bishop for the Middle District of the Mennonites. He was the Civil War Bishop of the Mennonites.

So I've got roots in Shenandoah, Rockingham, Augusta, Highland, Pocahontas, and Greenbrier. They all had been western Virginia counties.

I was raised in Fairfax County, Virginia. It would've been nicer to have been born here. But I've been here longer than I've been anywhere in my life.

John Heatwole's Artisan Ancestry

(1969-)	**David F. Heatwole**, painter and installation artist
(1948-)	**John L. Heatwole**, woodcarver and sculptor
(1883-1952)	**M.R. Preston**, cabinetmaker
(1860-1920)	**John T. Heatwole**, carpenter
(1826-1907)	**John D. Heatwole**, potter
(1843-1907)	**Peter Wine**, blacksmith
(1790-1859)	**Samuel Weaver II**, loom maker and weaver
(1796-1853)	**Andrew Coffman**, potter
(1817-1895)	**George Wine II**, carpenter
(? - ?)	**Joseph Curry**, cooper
(1797-1867)	**David Heatwole II**, carpenter
(1767-1840)	**David Heatwole**, shoe maker
(1774-1845)	**George Wine**, wagon maker
(1747-1812)	**Joseph Wenger**, loom maker
(? - ?)	**Christian Wenger**, rifle maker
(1747-1822)	**Michael Wine**, wagon maker
(1718-1794)	**Melchior Brenneman III**, weaver
(1717-1787)	**John Garber**, shoe maker
(? - ?)	**Andrew Kauffman**, weaver
(? - ?)	**Johann Georg Winn**, wagon maker
(1685-1749)	**Henrich Horn**, carpenter
(1680-1739)	**Jacob Wein**, shoemaker
(1665-1737)	**Melchior Brenneman II**, weaver
(1632-...?...)	**Melchior Brenneman**, weaver
(1615-1688)	**Georg Hutwhol**, cooper
(? - ?)	**Albrect Wein**, cabinetmaker

John carried this poster that he made around to his talks in order to illustrate his artisan heritage.

My mother's family came from over in Southern Maryland from Calvert County. I spent a lot of time over there as a child too. Eating crabs. Then as I got older I'd go out oyster tonging. It's a killer job. But I liked crabbing. Crabbing was so much fun.

CD: Do you have siblings?
JLH: I have one sister who's fifteen months older. She's a retired educator. I also have two step-brothers and two step-sisters.

My father, John L. Heatwole, Jr., and my mother, L. Marie Preston, had a rough marriage. He was a real sweet man, but he couldn't handle the way things were in their marriage. He left when I was about eight years old.

I had been coming back down here to the Shenandoah Valley and visiting with a great-uncle of mine, whose name was Paul Heatwole. I remembered him from when I was a child, he was such a great storyteller. He pretty much took me under his wing. He was more of a father to me than anybody ever was. He was a wonderful man. He told the best stories in the world and mostly family related stories.

CD: Is that where you learned about your ancestors?
JLH: Part of it. And then part of it, I just ferreted out myself. But he's the one that really got me started interviewing people. The stories were just so colorful.

John's artistic talents also manifested themselves in drawings as is seen in this eagle drawing done in preparation for a carving.

Courtesy JMU Special Collections

-Two-
Miriam
& Art Classes

"It has been the desire and pursuit of love that has held my imagination spellbound since my childhood."[4]

C**D:** How did you meet Miriam?

JLH: That's a funny story too. Like I said, I was always making things with my hands and painting. No training or anything. When I got to high school I took shop my freshman year and I was a poor kid. We had to do these drawings of furniture, all these different angles and everything. There were several guys in that class who just couldn't do it and hated it. They paid me five bucks and I'd do theirs for them. And it was so frustrating because they always got As and I always got Bs or Cs. (Laughter) But I got five bucks.

One day, one of the shop instructors came by and I wasn't paying attention. I don't even know what we were doing, but I was drawing in this little tablet that I carried with me, and he confiscated it from me and kept me after class. Mr. Litman, was his name, and he said, "These are pretty good drawings. You're not really much interested in the shop work, are you?"

I said, "No, it's really interesting, I kind of like it."

He said, "You know what I think would be better for you if you want to do it? Would you consider doing some murals for the shop wing? I'll pay for all the materials. You don't have to come to class. We'll have a classroom just for you where you can paint these big murals."

I said, "Okay, I'll do that."

So for two years, all I did was paint these murals for the shop wing. At the end of each year when they had the exam for shop, I'd have a shop teacher here and a shop teacher standing back here and they'd give me a multiple choice test with pictures. It would say, "Screwdriver," then there'd be a picture of a screwdriver and a hammer and a plane and I'd go to mark the hammer and they'd go, "Oh, it might not be that one." Until I got to the right one and then I'd check it. So I always got As in shop. (Laughter) This is true, this is true.

My sophomore year they built a new high school. A lot of us were transferring to that new high school for our junior year. The shop teachers wrangled it so that I skipped Art I & II and went into Art III. And the teacher, she hated me, "He doesn't have any art background." Just really ranting.

But that's where I met Miriam. The first day, I was late for class (laughter), walked in the class and Miriam was sitting there at a table. I was also a big jock. I played several positions: guard, tackle, linebacker. I played varsity for three years. One year at Woodson High School and two years at Thomas Jefferson High School, both in Fairfax County. In 1964 I was on the All State first team. In 1965 I was All District and All Northern Virginia. So I had my letterman's jacket on from the first school and I went and sat down at her table. I thought she was pretty interesting and I said, "Hi, I'm John Heatwole."

And she said, "So?" (Laughter)

CD: How to hook a man.

JLH: We dated on and off for a number of years. So that's how we met. In art class. At Jefferson High School. She had gone to Robert E. Lee High School. I had gone to Woodson High School, for our freshman and sophomore years. That's when we first met, in that art class.

I hated art class because the teacher hated me. We had a guy in the art class named Jim Montgomery who was probably the best person for his age that I've ever seen do art. He was

Miriam & John Heatwole, March 1983

phenomenal, he got a full scholarship to Pratt Art Institute in New York and ended up designing all these residences for people made out of old stables in New York City and all this beautiful work. She doted on him because she knew that he'd probably be famous and that would make her famous because she trained him. She couldn't teach him a thing.

It made me mad and the other kids too because she always doted on him. So the last class of my senior year, of course I was late for class like I always was, and she had told us ahead of time, "You're not going to have an exam." So I figured, "Why do I have to hurry to get there?" When I got there she said, "You're late. You're late for the exam." I asked, "What? You told us we weren't going to have an exam." She said, "Well, we are. It's just an essay. What you got out of this class." (Laughter)

I thought, oh boy, this is great, I can't wait. I did about four pages of how she played favorites and didn't know how to teach art. I got a B on it, for being honest. (Laughter)

CD: When did you start drawing?
JLH: I can't even remember when I first started.
CD: As a little tot?

JLH: Yes, a little tot, and I remember what I was doing too. Because my mother was raised a Catholic, she was from a really old Maryland family that came over on the Ark and the Dove. Catholic right down to the ends of their toenails.

I remember the first drawings I did were these little figure eights, thousands of them, but I put noses on them and little legs and arms and everything. I did scenes of the crucifixion. (Laughter) Tons of scenes of the crucifixion. Then I started doing little Civil War battles. Those were my first efforts, thank God none of them have survived.

CD: I would love to see the little figure eight drawings.

JLH: Oh no, no, they're awful. There are some people that actually have some early paintings that I did, that won't sell them back. Paintings I did when I was a teenager. They're just awful. Just terrible. You know how it is when you're a teenager, real dark. I did some awful stuff. (Laughter)

After high school, I went to college on an athletic scholarship and then got injured and couldn't afford to continue. After a stint in the Marine Corps, I worked for the Library of Congress for six years as a researcher. I liked it there and was doing pretty well but I never saw anything finished. As soon as you were finished with your part, it went to somebody else. You hardly ever really saw anything different, everything was pretty much by rote after a while.

There were glimpses of things that were kind of interesting. I straightened out a case for Edgar Rice Burroughs' son. He and I talked on the phone a lot and corresponded and he told me stories about his dad. How when his dad started writing, he was a traveling salesman. After "Tarzan of the Apes" came out he was able to make his living strictly by the writings. It's kind of neat. To have your own city, Tarzana, named after your writing.

-Three-
Sculpting

"What if I had never molded the creek clay into a human form as a child? And if friends and family had come easily? If I had never held a gouge and felt its power, or drawn upon paper images to be?"[5]

I have always done things with my hands. When I was probably seven, eight years old I started making figures out of clay that I would dig from a creek bank near my house. The only problem with that was, it was just all crumbly and everything.

One day I was walking along the creek bank looking for clay outcrops, I was maybe twelve or thirteen years old, and I ran into an older woman who was coming the other way wearing hip boots, with a sack over her shoulder. She said, "What are you doing?" I said, "Well, I'm digging some clay." She said, "Well, that's what I'm doing." She was a potter, Leona Morrow. She kind of took me under her wing and started to fire my things for me.

But it was just raw clay, and I'd try to mill it and get it cleaned and everything, but there was always pockets of sand or air bubbles. And nine times out of ten there'd be cracks or they'd actually blow up in the kiln while it was being fired.

When I was in my twenties, I decided to get into something that wouldn't blow up. (Laughter) And that's when I started carving the wood. I always carved anything that was carvable but had never really done much in the wood. I was checking into classes in the Washington area and some of them had wood sculpture, but it was involved with all these other things, macramé and other stuff I just wasn't interested in, at that time.

I saw an article in the newspaper about two old men that were church carvers and I called one of them up. I said, "I've been trying to learn from somebody how to use the tools. I'm willing to pay if somebody would just take me on." He said, "Well, I like the idea. Why don't you come out and we'll talk about it."

He lived in Clifton, which then, was way out in the boondocks. Now it's all built up around it. He lived at the end of the village. There was a long road that went back to the end of a spur of a hill. And a beautiful old house called Lone Oak Lodge. And a beautiful shop that looked out over all these farms. I think they're all gone now, that countryside. I worked with them for about six months. I had a special deal with the Library of Congress that I worked four days a week and that way I could have long weekends to go out with them.

I was twenty-four. Something like that. I learned really quick. They did a lot of bas relief and I was doing things in the round. I had showed them the things I did in clay beforehand and they said, "Well, we don't do anything like this. We don't know if...." And I said, "Well, I just really need to learn how to use the tools. That's the main thing."

They were just great, two great old men, Willard Webb and Don Stratton. Don Stratton always would be smoking a little short, stubby cigar, that never seemed to get any shorter. (Laughter) He just chewed on it a lot and smoked it once in a while. But when they passed away, they both left me some of their tools, so when I'm working with those tools, I always think back to those days up there with them. They were just great guys.

–Four–
Home to the
Shenandoah Valley

"The Shenandoah Valley is part of the Great Valley, a large region that stretches from New York to Alabama. In western Virginia, the Shenandoah Valley is between the Blue Ridge Mountains to the east and the Allegheny Mountains to the west. The Alleghenies are part of the Appalachian Mountain chain...."[6]

Finally I just got it into my head to come back to Rockingham County because I knew Virginia Craftsmen was here. I went to them and showed them the things that I had done while I was working with Willard and Don. The fellow that was running the place said, "Wow, these are really nice. Can you start tomorrow?" I said, "Well, no. I need to talk about salary." They said, "Well now, we can only pay you minimum wage, we have to start you at that because that's what everybody else started at. But we'll have you at a top salary within a year." Within a year, I was at top salary which I think was three dollars and ten cents an hour. (Laughter) It was 1975, I think. These employees were making gorgeous furniture, really beautiful stuff.

Carving, day after day, sometimes I would carve ten or fifteen fan carvings in a row. Or fifteen volutes on the ends of the backs of Windsor chairs, having to do that over and over again. I remember the first time I carved a fan carving. It must have taken me three or four days. After doing hundreds of them,

I could do one in probably twenty minutes. Just by rote, you end up knowing what your hands, your tools are going to do before you even think about it.

That's what was good about the place. The discipline of having to do that, day in and day out. It really paid off in the end.

There were just some great men working there. Some people that had so much talent, more talent in their little finger than most any wood-workers I've ever met. John Wissen-berger was a Windsor chair maker who has a shop in Winchester now. He had never made Windsor chairs before and he just fig-ured it out. He even built his own steam box to bend the things that needed to be bent

John Heatwole at his Bridgewater shop

on the Windsor chairs. He really made it into more of an art than I think anybody that had ever worked there. There were a lot of guys like that and most of them had been there twenty, thirty, forty years.

The first carvings I did professionally were after I left Virginia Craftsman. When you're working nine, ten hours a day there, it's hard to come home and free your mind up. I wanted to do figures. I wanted to do something that had some depth to it. And just couldn't do it.

Finally Miriam convinced me. I said, "I've gotta try to do this. Open a studio or something, and be able to try to do some things I really want to do. I think people will respond to them."

So I went to a wonderful lady in Bridgewater, Virginia, Evelyn Rowe, she had this little building. I took her some pictures of some things I'd carved earlier when I was still working with Willard Webb and Don Stratton. I said, "This is what I want to do. I want to carve wood. I want you to think about it. You're not doing anything with the building; you might never want to do anything with it, that's all right too. Let me leave these with you for a few days to think about it." She said, "Okay."

I came back a few days later and asked, "Have you given it some thought?" She said, "Yes. I'm enchanted with the idea. You can have the building." I asked, "What would you want to charge for rent?" She said, "You name the rent." I said, "Okay!"

I didn't know how I was going to do it or how long it was gonna take. I remember the first piece I sold took me a week to do and I sold it for twenty-five dollars. (Groan) It was the fall of '76.

I was working several different part time jobs for three years to make it work. Working all night and then coming home and sleeping and then going down there for six hours. Then I finally said, I've got to get these pieces somewhere where people don't care what they cost and up the prices, or somewhere where people understand the time that goes into hand carving something.

I had had some successes. I had sold pieces through a gallery, The Sporting Gallery, in Middleburg, Virginia. They took everything I could do pretty much, but it still wasn't enough as far as making what I needed to make.

-Five-
Neiman-
Marcus

The Washington Star covered the Neiman-Marcus show, which was a success, and called John, "The Wizard of Wood."[7]

One day I just packed up some things and went to Neiman-Marcus in Washington, D.C. Their manager was looking at the carvings and she said, "These are really wonderful, but I don't know what we can do with these. They're one of a kind. If we had forty of each one of them...."

I said, "No, I can't do that. I'm not ready to do something like that." I'm starting to pack them up, getting ready to leave, and their art director came in, Martin Zagaya, and he said, "Who did these?"

She said, "This fellow right here did them."

He looked at me and said, "Why don't you leave those for a few minutes and walk with me through the store. I want to talk to you about something."

We started walking through the store. The Neiman-Marcus in Washington is three stories and it's attached to this other part called Maza Galleria. The entrances are on the inside of this building to the three floors of Neiman-Marcus. They've got these windows that are about three feet square and maybe six feet tall. There's two of them at each entrance. He took me to all of these windows and said, "Do you have any ideas? I'm thinking about maybe commissioning you to do our Christmas windows for next year."

I said, "Oh." So I'm looking at the windows and just off the top of my head, I started... "How about this elf warehouse and some kind of a conveyance pulling packages, being pulled by a chipmunk and all these different things. Mushrooms out in the snow with elves dancing around them and all this kind of stuff."

He's going, "Yeah, yeah, yeah. Yeah, okay, yeah I like these." And then, "How much will it cost me?"

In my head, I'm going, oh man, I'm gonna price myself out of this. Or maybe it won't be enough. Finally I threw out a number and he said, "Okay, we'll do it." Shake hands. Then I said, "Now you'll probably want them sometime in early November or something."

He said, "No, this is Neiman-Marcus. We won't put them up until a week after Thanksgiving." I said, "Okay."

Martin said, "You do the figures. I'll set up woods and everything in these windows. I'll have a crew there the day you come to set it up."

I'm just thrilled to death that I'm gonna do this, but then I realize, "Oh no, I've committed to tons of little figures. Can I do this in six months?"

There was a picture in the *Daily News Record* of me when I had finished the windows, hadn't taken the pieces up yet, and

THE WIZARD OF WOOD

Neiman-Marcus is pleased to announce the artistry of Mr. John Heatwole, master woodcarver, in the Gift Galleries, December 4th thru 20th. Mr. Heatwole's sculptures, executed in native American hardwoods, run the scale from country folk and fantasy to stylized and realistic figures. Coming from a direct line of Shenandoah Valley artisans, the artist's work stands alone in its medium as he produces one of a kind pieces using only hand tools.
Come see this unique artisan and share in his imagination!

**Neiman-Marcus notice from John's first exhibit there.
The carving is of Elizabeth Heatwole.**

I looked like a raccoon because I had worked seven days a week, about fourteen hours a day. I think I still have that somewhere. I mean, I did, I looked just like a raccoon, the darkest circles. Like somebody had hit me in both eyes as hard as they could. But anyway, got them up there and he was true to his word. He had this crew of about three or four people, to set them up. And they started setting them up, right away. I don't know where they had gotten them, but they had cut branches that looked like trees that were kind of disappearing in the tops of these things and the snow looked real. Then they started setting them up and Martin said to one of the other people, "Go upstairs and get Dee." She was the manager of the store that I had talked to, almost a year earlier.

She comes down and she's looking at them and her eyes are just getting big and she said, "How would you like to do a one-man show here?" She said, "It will last for a week. We'll close down the store for the night, for the opening."

I said, "Okay! When do you want to do it?" And remember this is the first of December.

She said, "How about May 30th?" That was five months off.

I said, "Okay, that sounds good. How many pieces do you want?"

She said, "How about fifty?"

I said, "Okay, I'll do fifty pieces." So again it was raccoon time all over again. (Laughter)

I got forty-eight pieces done. That was really good. Then when I took them there for them to set up for the show, she was asking me to help her price them. I said, "A hundred and fifty for this, two hundred for whatever."

She said, "We'll double all of these."

I said, "Double? They'll never sell at that."

"You let us worry about that part," was her answer.

The first show, I think we sold twenty-eight or something like that, and I was kind of disappointed. She said, "Don't worry about it, the next one, we'll sell them all." She said, "I want you to do a show for Christmas this year."

Again, it's the end of May, so it's five and a half months. I had maybe another two weeks or something longer than before. And the next show, we did sell out.

I was so tired, because really it had been almost two years of constantly carving, mostly for them, and trying to live off of the other things that I was selling. The checks were good from them, but I couldn't live the whole year on it.

So when she said, "Okay. We'll just do it like last time. We'll do May and then we'll do December." I said, "I can't. Let's just do December. It will give me more time. I'll do better work." I love working under pressure because I feel like I do good work, but I didn't think I could physically keep doing it.

We sold out that next December show, too. Yeah, May, December and then December, December. We did five shows all together.

It was a lot of fun. It was really kind of spectacular to see these people coming in from all walks of life.

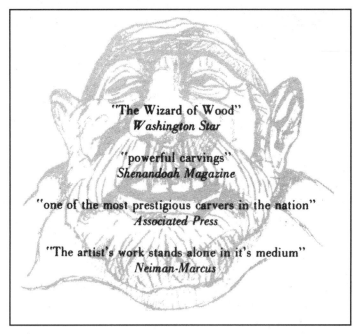

"The Wizard of Wood"
Washington Star

"powerful carvings"
Shenandoah Magazine

"one of the most prestigious carvers in the nation"
Associated Press

"The artist's work stands alone in it's medium"
Neiman-Marcus

The back of a Neiman-Marcus invitation

-Six-
Colorful
People

"Who knows what invisible threads tie into every soul, every creature."[8]

The people I didn't sell to are the more interesting people. (Laughter) Well, some of the ones I sold to are pretty interesting, too.

This one young woman came in and she was raving about the carvings. She said, "I'm going to bring my mother over because she'll be interested in these."

She brings her mother over, and her mother, definitely Middle Eastern in all these beautiful robes, I can't even describe the garment she was wearing. She's looking and she says, "Oh, these really are nice, how much are they?" And I gave her the price list that they had for the Neiman-Marcus opening; this was the next day.

She said, "Oh, they're very nice but they're just so expensive." So she and her daughter go over to the silver section and she spends eighteen-thousand dollars on a tray that has a lobster top on it. It looked like a real lobster.

Found out later she was the sister of the King of Saudi Arabia. (Laughter) She could have bought the whole darn show! I guess because they were wood. She wanted precious metals and gemstones or something. I should have done a Buddha, no, that wouldn't have worked with her, but with a big ruby in its navel or something. (Laughter)

The funniest thing that ever happened, again, involved a young girl. She must have been maybe ten or eleven, and she's looking. There was one especially that she liked. It was all out of one piece of wood and it was this little man walking a duck on a little leash. The base and everything, all one piece. It was kind of a fun piece. She's looking at it and there were others in that particular case. I asked, "Which do you like the most?"

She said, "I really like that man walking the duck."

I said, "That's one of my favorites too." Very seldom do I get an idea in my head and it comes out looking exactly like I thought, but this one was real close to that.

She said, "I think I'm gonna buy it."

I said, "Little girl, I'm sorry, but that's six hundred dollars."

She says, "Okay." And she pulls out this wad of bills and starts peeling them off.

I said, "No, no, no. Don't pay me. You pay these sales people over here." (Laughter)

The sales people had told me in the beginning, "There will be people that come in here that you don't think have two nickels to rub together, but they might be millionaires."

The little girl buys the man walking the duck and then comes back a little while later with her mother, who is this really gorgeous woman. Probably about, at that time, maybe in her fifties. Her hair was just beautifully coifed and everything. They're looking around and she spends about another two thousand dollars, buys a few more carvings. So that worked out real well.

And then the next year, I get a call from the mother, and she says, "Are you going to be at Neiman-Marcus again?" I said, "Yes."

She said, "Because I want to bring my husband and have him look at your pieces too."

"Oh, that's great."

She shows up; he doesn't show up, but she buys a couple more carvings and takes them away. They lived out in Potomac, Maryland.

Probably 1984 or '85, John Wissenberger and Ray Pine and I got together and we had a group show at the Augusta Art

Center at Gypsy Hill Park in Staunton, Virginia. It's furniture and chairs and then my carvings.

Well, it's opening day, and of course all the people are coming in and everything, and then I see this stretch limousine pull up out front.

I should have mentioned the woman is fairly tall, she's about five-ten, very elegant. (Laughter) The chauffeur comes out and opens the door and out steps this nice looking young man and then out steps the mother and the daughter. Then this little, short, bald guy smoking a cigar. They come in and I said, "I can't believe you made it all the way down here."

She said, "I wouldn't have missed it for the world. We brought our interior decorator, Richard." She said, "I want you to meet my husband. He gave up a Redskins game to come down for this." (Laughter)

This little bald guy with the cigar says, (mafia accent), "Mr. Heatwole, I'm really glad to meet you. My wife has told me all about your stuff and I want to see what you got here. We're thinking about adding a room to the house for your stuff." (Laughter)

I met some really interesting characters.

Ben Bradley walked through one time, leading his Irish wolfhound. Martin Agronsky bought a piece, you probably remember him, he was an old commentator that used to be one of the Sunday morning talk show hosts.

The closest I ever got to a President was to Reagan, his masseur. He came in and he bought a piece. He was telling me about Reagan, he said he was a real nice guy. He said, "He jokes around a lot when I start working on him and then he falls asleep."

One other interesting thing. Years ago I had a knock on the door of the studio. I closed the studio down probably within three years because I couldn't get any work done when the blinds were up, people were always stopping by the shop in Bridgewater. Busses would stop, I don't know where they came from, it was just strange. They just wanted to look. They didn't want to buy anything. They just wanted to see this quaint guy carving.

One day two old ladies came by, and I'm in there carving and they said, "Hi! When will the wood carver be back?"

I said, "Well, I'm the wood carver."

They said, "No, no, no. We mean your father, or your grandfather."

I said, "No, I'm the wood carver."

Courtesy JMU Special Collections

"Playing Checkers" by John Heatwole

They said, "You're John Heatwole?"

I said, "Yes."

"We thought you'd be an old man." (Laughter) This is twenty years ago and I wasn't an old man yet.

Another day I had a knock at the door and it was a fellow from Gabon in Africa. We just sat and talked about woods, for a couple hours, something like that. About two months later, this package comes and it's just full of little blocks, nice size blocks of wood. Hard as a rock. They were all labeled, babinga and padauck and all these different kinds of wood.

I did a wounded Viking out of one piece, kneeling down, leaning on his shield, out of one of those woods. This man with

**"Wounded Viking" by
John Heatwole, 1979**

a British accent comes up to me at one of the Neiman-Marcus shows and is looking at it. He says, "I've always been so fascinated with the Scandinavian Viking culture. I want to purchase that piece for my collection." "Okay." So all this time, I'm thinking he's some guy from Oxford or something, and he was the military attaché to the Jordanian Embassy. He was actually a Jordanian, he was a major. I've always wondered what happened to him, Timor Dagastani, was his name. He must have been brought up in England or went to school there because his accent was flawless English. You didn't hear any other kind of inflection in it at all.

That was fun, the Neiman-Marcus years. Five years I did those. I did the windows for three years. Finally I said, "Look. Let's just do the shows. I can't do the windows. You need somebody else doing them for a change." (Laughter) That was a lot of fun.

-Seven-
Sickness &
the U.S. Senate
Rotunda show

*"When the pressure starts getting to me, I some-
times wonder what my life would have been like if
I had chosen another path to explore. I know the
path I chose was correct and that I'll spend my life
defining it and redefining it."9*

Every year after that I did one or two gallery shows where it was either a one man or two or three people. I did those because I always knew I would pick up two or three more collectors that I'd be able to sell to outside of doing those shows. You had to live off of what you'd already made while you're getting ready for the next show.

I did that for a while, and then I think in '85, I was chosen to be in this show that lasted for a month at the Delaware Art Museum. They did the first fantasy art show in America. They picked eighteen artists from around the world, out of the group there were maybe seven or eight Americans and the rest were from overseas. Some of them were getting fairly well known, even by that time, and have gotten even more well known since.

One of the main artists for the recent *Lord of the Rings* Trilogy, John Howe, he was one of the them. He was from England and Switzerland. He lived in Switzerland. And Brian Froud, a lot of movies have been done where he's designed all the stuff for them. The most well known and the one I got closest to was Ray Harryhousen.

The Delaware Art Museum people said that it was the most

well attended show that they'd ever had. It was wonderful. These huge, huge banners and lines and lines of people. It was really neat.

Then they had another one and again it was all juried. They invited back the original people from the first show and then they added about ten more. So they did another show in '89.

Courtesy JMU Special Collections

"Man before his fall" by John Heatwole

That was a lot of fun, too.

Then I got really sick. I was getting sick at about that time. I was having trouble with my colon, weren't sure what it was, all this stuff going on. I was in and out of the hospital, '89, '90. Probably about six months all told, for those two years. Then in '91 it got so bad that I had to go in almost permanently for three months straight through.

The first day we go into the hospital in 1991, which was January 3rd or something, Miriam goes home to get some stuff. She comes back and she said, "When I was going out the door, the phone was ringing. The United States Senate wants you to do a one man show in their Rotunda on Capitol Hill."

I said, "Oh no, Miriam, shut up."

She said, "No, they really do. They really want you to do a show."

I said, "Are you serious?"

She said, "Yes. The phone rang and that's who it was, a guy from one of the Senator's offices." I finally ended up talking to that guy while I was in the hospital.

As time went on, by March, I knew there was no way I was going to be able to do it. So I called them up from the hospital and I just said, "I'm just still too sick, and it's going to be a long recovery. Could we do it later in the year?" I think we set it up for November.

I got out of the hospital at the end of March and went home. I had to sleep downstairs for probably about six months because I just couldn't go upstairs after having my colon removed, which was awful. I threw blood clots right and left and they thought I was going to die. It was really awful.

The first day I went out of the house and walked just to the end of the street, which is maybe sixty yards, I felt like I had run a marathon. I felt great and worn out at the same time.

So we went ahead and left that scheduled for November. They wanted it up for three weeks or a month, I can't remember which. Since I was home all the time (laughter), I wasn't going even to the studio, I started calling people to borrow pieces back for this show. They had sent me diagrams of the Rotunda and everything.

My friend, Randy Stover, who runs Mill Cabinet Shop, in Bridgewater, he made a bunch of display stands that could be broken down, so they can just be taken all flat and then we'd put them together once we got there. So he did that and then the day came to take it up. Jim Swope of Bridgewater came along with Randy to help set up the show.

The Senator's office had told me, "When you come up here, you're going to have to go through all these checkpoints before you even get to the building." Oh gad, this is gonna be great. I felt like I was gonna die, I felt so sick.

The first night, we got almost to Washington and stayed at a hotel. They had their rooms, I had my room. When we got there, we hadn't had supper yet, and I just gave them some money and I said, "Just go have supper. I'll either see you in the morning or you'll just have to carry me out and bury me. I'm so sick. I'm either gonna be well tomorrow or I'm gonna be dead."

I just went up to the room and tried to get to sleep, and the next morning I felt great. The day before I just really felt awful.

We had to go through two places away from the Capitol to have the vans scanned with dogs and mirrors. We had to have all that checked. Finally we got to the Rotunda and we had to be checked again. Once we cleared that, we put everything on three big carts, and looked down this hall. The guard said, "Go down there and you'll see the signs for how to get there."

The hall, I think, is a mile long. I could hardly walk. I had a walking stick. I get to the end of it, turn, and it's going that way for a mile more. (Laughter) By the time we got up there, I was almost out of it again. I was so tired because I hadn't done any kind of walking like that.

We got it all set up. Senator Warner was the original sponsor of it. It had to go before the Senate to okay this thing. Other Senators came and looked at it once it was up. Just kind of looked at it and went away.

I remember Joe Biden stopped and commented and said, "Hey, this is really nice. Are you the artist?" That was interesting, nice guy.

I think we stayed the next day and left in the afternoon of the next day. But at one point, Randy Stover and Jim Swope had gone somewhere, I don't know where, and I was kind of alone in there, except for the guards. Some guy came in and he was saying, "Is this your work?"

I said, "Yes."

He said, "Well, this is really nice." Then he said, "Well, how did you get this gig?"

I said, "I didn't really get it. Somebody saw an article in *Fine Woodworking Magazine* and thought it would be nice to show my work at the Capitol, so they asked me to do it."

He said, "You didn't have to twist their arms to do it?"
I said, "No."

He went berserk. He's yelling and screaming, "How come you get to come in here and nobody else does?" He's screaming and the guards swooped down on him and hauled him out of the place. (Laughter) It was so bizarre. I thought he was going to pull a gun and start shooting or something. It was really weird, but anyway, it all worked out.

Then Miriam, she was the activities director at that time for Heritage Haven at Virginia Mennonite Retirement Community. She took a busload of her people up to see the White House, and to see some other things, and to go to this show, too. That was nice, except her boss brought on the bus that morning, prune juice and bran muffins. For all these old folks. And Miriam said it was awful. She said, "We were at the White House and they didn't have any public bathrooms. These people had to go." They had to go across the street, through a security check. It was really embarrassing.

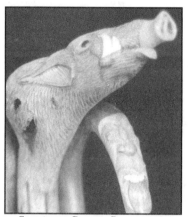

Courtesy Bruce Rossenwasser
**Carved cane handles
by John Heatwole**

She said that this one little old lady that she really, really enjoyed, they had just seen the show at the Rotunda and they got on an elevator to go back down to where they parked. And it opened up another time and Ted Kennedy gets on. Of course he turns around and is facing out toward the door. (Laughter) So this little old woman kept pinching Miriam real hard, and pointing, and Miriam is trying to get her hand off because she's just making her black and blue. Finally Kennedy gets off and Miriam said before he was even three steps away, the older woman said, "You know, he doesn't look as bad as he looks on TV." (Laughter)

Great stuff like that happens all the time to us. That was a real thrill for her.

After that I think I only did one more one man show at a gallery in Annapolis. I did that with my son, David. David is a painter, sculptor, and installation artist. He's become known for large outdoor installations covering acres of ground. His last big commission was reproducing the logo of the Frederick County Maryland Arts Commission with PVC pipe and painted sheets covering a large portion of a park in Frederick. That was in 1992, that was the last one man show that I did. I had gotten so tired of it. I had enough work; it was all word of mouth. I had commissions, most of the time, almost a year ahead.

I keep thinking I should do another one sometime, I don't know if I could do it. Well, I am gonna do one at the end of May for four months at the Historical Society Museum in Dayton, Virginia. So I'll borrow back a bunch of pieces for that.

The only thing I'm not going to do like that show at

This Heatwole (father and son) exhibition postcard featured a pen and ink drawing on the left drawn from a bronze by John Heatwole. The pencil drawing on the right is by David Heatwole.

Courtesy of Bruce
Rossenwasser

**Finger drum
carved in 1996**

the Rotunda, is borrow back pieces from all over the country. They were all insured, but I had to get everything back to the people too. It just took forever. So I'm just going to borrow local pieces.

CD: I used to work with Milton and Betty Coyle, they have some of your work.

JLH: Yes, they have some pieces. I'm glad you mentioned that, because I'm going to forget some people. I'm just gonna borrow one or two pieces from people here and there. I need to write that down and call them too because I've got to start putting that together pretty soon.

CD: Another one I know of is Bruce Rossenwasser.

JLH: Yes. I want to call him because he's got this little drum thing that I made that I really like. I'm gonna try and borrow that back from him. I also have some bear feet of his here. Not real bears. These old carved wooden ones that guys used to use to throw still hunters off with the track of bears. (Laughter) I've had those now for about a year, I've got to talk to Bruce, get those back to him.

Dr. Deyerle was one of my earliest collectors. He had about three hundred pieces when he died.

-Eight-
Shenandoah Voices, The Burning, & Beyond

"The thing that impressed me the most was the visual type of things that came out of those oral histories. A woman talking about looking south toward where that burning was coming from. And the sky being very low and all these columns of smoke looking like they were holding the sky up from falling down."[10]

After the Rotunda show, I started thinking about all these interviews and stories that I had collected and I should do something with this because I might not be here for too much longer. That's why I wrote the first book, *Shenandoah Voices* [Rockbridge Publishing Company, Berryville, Virginia, 1995].

I started working on it right after that. I did the first book all in longhand on yellow legal pads. I must have had a stack of forty of those things. Every once in a while, I'd get them mixed up or leave one in another room and be pulling my hair out trying to move things around within the chapters. Oh, that was a nightmare.

Then with the second book, which was *The Burning* [Rockbridge Publishing, imprint of Howell Press, Charlottesville, Virginia, 1998], I started out using the legal pads. I said, "No, this is stupid. I've got to get a computer." Somebody had an old 2.5 or something, it was a really ancient computer, and that was a nightmare using that computer, all these glitches. Then I got a word processor, and then I finally got this computer which works fine. I'm okay with that, except if I try to get creative and try to play with something I don't know anything about. I try not to do that at all. (Laughter) It really is a godsend having that.

The second book, as you know, was about the burning of the Shenandoah Valley by Sheridan's troops in the fall of 1864. The reason I did that one was because for years I had known about this, and read what little there was about it.

Usually when I interview people I look at census records later to see how what they've told me about their family members ties into the stories. The other thing I do is, if they have family genealogies, I look through them too.

During the interviews, it seemed like everybody had a story about the burning. When I got the genealogies, even if they were straight, black and white, who married whom, and how many kids they had and what church they went to and when they died and where they were buried: if there was one story, nine times out of ten, it was about the burning of the Valley, in the fall of 1864.

So I thought, this has got to be a really important event. The history books of that period barely made mention of it. If there was a paragraph, that was a lot. Sometimes they didn't even mention it at all. Going through some of the regimental histories, a lot of times they didn't mention it at all, and these were the troops involved and actually doing the burning.

The first person who got it right was a fellow from Pennsylvania named Jeffry Wert, who's written about ten books on the Civil War. He said that this was a thirteen-day campaign to bring the Valley pretty much to its knees so that the Confederate Army could not operate here, and so supplies could not leave here to go to resupply Lee's army around Petersburg. Everything else that I had read, even by such noted historians as Bruce Catton, James MacPherson, all of them said it was three days.

As I started doing more and more research I realized it was thirteen continuous days, not three. Plus a lot of times they had it in the wrong time. Catton said that it started ten days after the Battle of Cedar Creek, when in reality by the Battle of Cedar Creek, it had been over for ten days. People kept picking up Catton's writings and would reuse that without checking the records.

Another part of it was that it was full of what I love the most and that's those small, wonderful stories that people pass down in their families.

Some historians, when I contacted them for advice, when I told them what I was doing, that I was mixing not only the documentary evidence but also the oral histories, they said, "Oh, you can't do that, that won't be accepted, because it's oral history. It changes and everything."

In the beginning of the book I mention that a lot of this is made up of oral history traditions from families, but there's a kernel of truth there. If nothing else, it's the emotions that that family felt when it was happening that comes through the story whether it happened exactly that way or not. In some cases I could actually research it and find out whether it really did happen or not. A couple of families, I had to tell them, the way you told it, couldn't have happened because of this, this, and this, and they hated that.

My name is Mud in this county with one family because they had a tradition that a future president was the one that led one of the burning parties. He wasn't here at that time, but he was a young man, there were a lot of young men that looked the same at that time. They had seen a picture of him thirty years later in a newspaper. "Oh, that's him, that's the man that burned our barn." That kind of thing.

I was really pleasantly surprised when *The Burning* came out and it was received really well. Actually it's gotten about thirty national reviews and all of them have been really good reviews.

And then it got one. (Laughter) A woman in New York wrote this review and just hated the book. I'm trying to figure out if I ever dated her or something. Because it was really personal, it was so weird. And all the rest of them were so good.

In fact this guy came up to me at a book signing and said, "You know your book was just reviewed in *Civil War News*." I went, "Oh NO!" He asked, "What do you mean, oh no?" I said, "I've read their reviews, they cut people to ribbons."

One of the reviews that I'd read the month before, I can't even remember what the book was, but the reviewer said, "This book belongs on the ash heap of history." (Laughter) I prayed, "Oh please, don't ever let them review one of my books," but it was a good review.

Then this one from this woman was just awful. It really was kind of vitriolic and I thought, "Man, I must have met her somewhere and did something I shouldn't have." I don't know. So I've got this one and thirty others. (Laughter)

The nice thing about doing something like that is after it's done and people read it, so many other stories come out of the woodwork.

I was talking to a man at the bottom of the hill a few nights ago. There's a house over here that I've been researching, called "Wheatlands." Beautiful brick house. As the crow flies, less than a mile away, was the home of Jackson's chief engineer, whose name was Claiborne Mason. Interesting guy, was maybe dyslexic or something. He was illiterate and yet he was an engineer. When these college trained engineers couldn't figure something out, he would figure it out and they would get going. In Bridgewater he built a bridge while the others were scratching their heads. I found out that at that house, there was a barn where they were storing Confederate uniforms and the soldiers burned it to the ground with all the wool uniforms inside it.

That would have been a great one for the book. You think about that and think, "Well, someday." First you want to correct any mistakes you made in the book, and then you can add these new stories to it too, and just expand the book. That's what I think Robert Tanner did who wrote the first book about Stonewall Jackson, or the most lengthy modern research book about Jackson's 1862 Valley campaign. He wrote that book twenty years ago and then just came out with a new edition which is this thick (stretches thumb and forefinger apart), with everything that he found since then.

That's down the road a little bit, but I'm looking forward to doing that. I'm working on two other books right now. But you know, it's just getting it done. There's not enough time.

CD: How long did *The Burning* take to write?
JLH: Research, maybe about two-and-a-half, three years. Until I felt like, okay, this is it, I've got to write it. Then it took me less than a year to write it. Probably about seven months.

CD: There's a phenomenal amount of research, to dig that information up. How did you go about that?
JLH: To get it straight too. That was the hardest part, to try to do it in chronological order because on all those thirteen days, sometimes there was more burning going on in one area than another. Sometimes there was burning going on in Page County while there was still burning going on in Rockingham. Trying to keep all that straight so that people didn't get lost. That was the hardest part, I think.

The rest of it, I did file cards and would move them around and see what looked like it was the most logical way to proceed with it.

The odd thing about it, and you've probably run into this too when you've been writing, a lot of times when it's over and months later I'm looking back and think, "How did that happen?" I'll look at it and think, "I don't have that kind of discipline. I couldn't have done that." (Laughter)

That's the problem, where I am right now. This past year has just been so wild. You knew about the cancer. In 2003 I was diagnosed with kidney cancer. In September of that year my right kidney was removed over at U.Va. [University of Virginia] Hospital. Besides the large tumor attached to the outside of the kidney, they found two more inside. I'm now down to three-month visits to monitor the other kidney.

I have two books to write and finish work on. One is another folklore book. This goes into detail about the nineteenth and early twentieth-century belief in witches in the uplands of Virginia and West Virginia. The other book is about irregular warfare in the Valley and the northeastern counties of West Virginia during the Civil War.

I wrote hardly anything on those books; probably not anything for six months or more. Last night I was thinking, tonight, maybe, or tomorrow night, or the night after, I'm going to start; every night for two hours. I've done the research, I just have to write it.

That's where I am now. And then the carvings, that's the other thing I didn't tell you. From 1979 probably to '86 or '87, I did about a hundred pieces a year in carvings. That's a lot. It really did wear me out. Now I do about thirty pieces a year. Times have changed. I'm not getting twenty-five or fifty dollars for a week's work. That helps a lot too. I love doing it and I'm looking forward to the day when I can just do it when I want to and what I want to do and keep it.

My son, David, and my daughter-in-law, they each get a piece at Christmas. But there's a lot of pieces that are gone that I wish we still had.

Nine

John's Tools

"There is a certain magic about the wood and in-struments that makes me feel more complete than the universe."[11]

One of the other things, and you can see it looking around this room, I just love artifacts. Things. Tools. A lot of tools that were used for different things. Things that have to do with family. Behind you is the Indian warning bell from the Heatwole log cabin. That's the cabin of my great-great-great-great grand-mother. She was just saved from being killed during the Wyoming massacre, because one of her brothers, who was already wounded, put her in a canoe and pushed her out into the middle of the Susquehanna River. She was laying down in it. She said, when she got to the other side, there was bark all over her back from where the rifle balls that the Indians were shooting at her had hit the canoe. That was hung outside of their cabin which is only, from the courthouse in Harrisonburg, it was out in the country at one time, but it's as the crow flies, about a mile-and-a-quarter from Harrisonburg, Virginia.

I got that warning bell and brought it home. Actually it was kind of a generic thing. They would hang it from the limb of a tree outside of a cabin and they'd have a signal that they would beat on it with a piece of hard wood or a piece of metal if it was time to come in to eat, when the hands were working in the fields, or there'd be another signal if the cabin was on fire, something like that. And then a signal if there were Indians in the area.

There's that one and the little piece of one right there that broke, is actually from Bridgewater, from a field just at the edge of town, it was plowed up.

The tools. There's corn shucking pegs and reaping hooks and all tools of early America that come from the counties here in the Valley. You know, those are stories too.

For a long time, my biggest collection was corn shuckin' pegs. The little things on the wall, are all corn shuckin' pegs. There's a couple over here too.

They just go on the inside of your fingers. There's a loop that goes around your middle fingers and you push against that with your thumb when you get the leaves at the top of the ear of corn. You can pull them down easier without making your fingers real sore and rough. I've always thought that that was the most important tool in early America. First of all you had to shuck the corn to get it ready to feed to your livestock, but it was also one of the most important social gatherings for people that didn't see each other all that much. They'd come from farm to farm to be together.

I've only interviewed one person, and she died last year, Doreen Ralston, who remembered going to corn shuckin' bees. Everybody else said, "Well, that was before my time, but we heard about it from our parents." She said that where she lived in Highland County that they still did it up into the 1920s. She said her father, every spring would plant his corn and he'd always have red ears because he'd plant those red seed corn. Everybody knew, Mr. Ralston was gonna have a lot of red ears of corn, because if you found a red ear, supposedly you could kiss anybody you wanted to at the corn husking.

I asked, "Doreen, did you do a lot of kissing at those corn huskings?"

She said, "No, I didn't. My girlfriends and I were sour on kissing. All those boys chewed tobacco." (Laughter)

She also said that the people would bring banjoes and fiddles. She remembered some of the songs, she didn't remember them all but she remembered snatches of them and she sang them to me.

Courtesy JMU Special Collections

John with his woodcarving tools, 1985

One of them was: (John sings) MacDonald had an old gray mule, and he drove him around in a cart, he loved that mule and that mule loved him, with all his mulish heart. (Laughter)

She said there were more stanzas than that to it. I've never found that one anywhere. There was another one she talked about taking tobacco to Lynchburg. She had two or three stanzas of that. I did find that song in one of the old folksong books. She was a great, great interview.

Like I said, other people, even her age, here in the main Valley, didn't remember actually being at corn husking bees.

They said, "No. When we were growing up they would hire people to come in." Every once in a while a neighbor would come in or they'd just shuck it at the field and not bring it all into the barn and have a party.

One woman talked about hiring all the people out at the poor house. They'd come in and shuck corn for a couple of days, and then they'd go back to the poor house.

It's so unbelievable the different things they used. Bone. Those two over there, the top one is bone and the other one is bone too. With leather straps on them. Up here, there are a couple of deer spikes, antler spikes. They're made out of all kinds of different things.

Some of the tools are really so odd that very few people remember them anymore. Like that little tiny ski over on the wall there. They used to strap it to their shoes, and that way when the barnyard was real muddy they could just kind of skate across the mud. (Laughter) So it's called a mud ski.

There's a scalping knife up there and a tomahawk, and a long knife.

When I was growing up, you're not as old as I am, but in cowboy movies, the Indians would always talk about the long knives. Everybody thought, "That means the cavalry with their sabers." Actually the long knives were the Virginians carrying those long fighting knives. That one's from here in Augusta County. The Virginia Militia.

I've done carvings that have to do with some of the stories I heard from people growing up. Other things just have to do with things I remember in my childhood or things that I imagined. It's kind of a mixture of things.

I think that's what I would do if I could just retire and do the kind of things I want to do. I'd do a lot of things from the Valley stories.

-Ten-
Uncle Paul

"In the Shenandoah Valley, the first sheep shearing of the year usually takes place soon after the first of May. The old timers say that a cold rain will follow within a few days of the shearing — a "sheep rain." People used to use the sheep rain as a date to plan other events around. Someone might say, 'Let's register that deed at the courthouse before the "sheep rain"' or, 'We'll be married after the sheep rain.'"[12]

C **D:** How old were you when you first met your Uncle Paul?

JLH: When I was a child. But when I started coming back here, I was in my early twenties, just riding around, and knowing it was kind of home, but not really knowing anybody, where they lived or anything, and didn't want to just drop in.

One day I just called him and I said, "Look, I'm coming down to the Valley, would you mind if I stopped in to see you?" "Oh no, come on by." That was the start of everything.

It was really kind of strange too because he knew that I wanted to come back to the Valley. I was really doing well at the Library of Congress. I was a GS-9 and they had promised that if I wouldn't leave, I would be an eleven within a few weeks. I said, "No, I've got to go. I just really feel like I've got to do that."

When I came down here and found out what Virginia Craftsman said they were gonna pay me, I called Miriam up and told her what they had said. She said, "It's up to you. I know you want to do this and you might always wonder if you don't."

Uncle Paul said, "Money's not everything. There's quality of life too." That was a big help in making that decision.

He was good with advice. He never really made a lot of money but he was one of the happiest people that I had ever met. And the stories, I just fell in love with those stories.

Some of the first stories that Uncle Paul ever told me were about this blacksmith that lived at Rushville who had married into the Heatwole family. His name was Ben Southard. The stories were just such wonderful tall tales and of course he swore they were all true.

One of the first ones was, he said, that Ben could sell anything. But he had a brother-in-law who was always losing his shirt, getting involved in all these business ventures and just didn't know how to sell. So one day he came to Ben's blacksmith shop and he said, "Ben, I've contracted with the Purina people. They've got this new laying mash. I'll tell you what, if you'll sell it for me, because you're the salesman of the family, you don't have to invest a nickel in it and you can have half the profits." So Ben said, "Well, can I do it of an evening after I close down the shop?" He said, "Yeah, you can sell it whenever you want to." So Ben said, "Okay, I'll give it a try for a while."

So the first night he was gonna try it, he closed down the blacksmith shop and loaded the bags of laying mash onto the back of his buckboard and he would go around to all the farms.

Everybody knew him but he had a spiel. His spiel was, he'd knock on the door and the farmer would come to the door and he'd say, "Hello there. I'm Ben Southard and I represent the Purina folks. We've got this new laying mash. You mix it up with your regular chicken feed, the chickens take a bite of it, tighten up their lips, curl up their toes and fill the atmosphere with eggs." (Laughter)

They said by the end of the first day he'd sold every bag of it. There's a whole bunch of stories like that about Ben Southard and they're all wonderful. They're funny. He was a neat guy.

One he told on my grandfather. My grandfather was

somebody else who I hadn't seen for years. He was the one that was the big success; made all the money in Washington. All I can remember about him was him sitting and counting money. No sense of romance or adventure. I did start seeing him again.

Great-uncle Paul Heatwole

One time, I was down here and Uncle Paul was telling me a story. He said, "You know, your grandfather hated the country. He hated going out every morning and milking the cows, and going up in the mountains during the summertime with the cattle, to stay with them. But he loved to play baseball." He said, "He was one of the best pitchers ever to come out of Rockingham County. He was so good that sometimes the pros would even send guys down to try to bat off of him. He had a curveball that was unbelievable. He'd throw that ball and it looked like it was gonna go right across the plate. The batter would swing at it and the ball would break and go behind the batter's back."

I said, "What?"

He said, "Yep, it would get almost to the plate and it would break and go behind the batter's back and he'd swing."

I said, "That doesn't sound possible."

He said, "I swear, your grandfather could do that." (Laughter)

So my grandfather was down visiting one time and I had the two of them sitting at the table. These two old white, white, white haired old gentlemen. And I was gonna try to embarrass Uncle Paul. So I said, "Granddaddy, Uncle Paul told me this story about,..."

For one thing, he hated Uncle Paul's stories, "Oh! He's such a liar." Bla, bla, bla and all this kind of stuff. Hated Uncle Paul's stories.

So I was gonna embarrass Uncle Paul. I said, "Granddad, Uncle Paul told me that you were a baseball pitcher for Clover Hill for quite a while."

He said, "Yep. I pitched baseball for Clover Hill."

I said, "He told me that you could throw this curveball that would almost get to the plate and break and go behind the batter's back and he'd swing."

I figured he was gonna say, "Well Paul, you're a damned liar." He kind of thought for a minute and he said, "Yep. I could do that. One morning I went out to milk the cows, a cow kicked me in the elbow and ruined my career." (Agonized laughter.)

So here I am. You know my grandfather's just real serious and never funning about anything and here he says, "Yeah, I could do that." Can anybody do that?

CD: (Laughter) No kidding. Did he pass that on, teach it to anybody?

JLH: He should have been a pitching coach for the pros. Of course, he couldn't have shown them anymore because of that cow.

All of Uncle Paul's stories were great like that. They always had wonderful endings, and of course, I kind of supplied the ending to that one with, "Yeah, I could do that."

Unfortunately, I only have one recording of my late Uncle Paul. We usually just sat, or walked and talked.

−Eleven−
Folklore
Interviews

"When I am gone, I will probably be spoken of as one who lived in memory but more, I hope that I'll be remembered as one who created them."[13]

The stories that Uncle Paul told were the kind of things that made me realize that other people had stories, too. So that's when I started going out, first in the Dry River community where they were from, and interviewing people that they had talked about or whose families they had talked about. And I found those stories just as rich, if not richer than the ones he told.

CD: Did you start taping or write it down or just put it in your head?

JLH: Actually, in the early days, I took some notes but not a whole lot. I didn't tape at all. When I first started interviewing Uncle Paul and by the mid-seventies I was writing everything down and dating it. Putting it on cards. All those things up there have cards in them and there's some in these files too. (Pointing to the file cabinets at the end of the room.) So there are literally hundreds of them.

I should have taped earlier but the mid-nineties is when I started doing the tapes.

It's good to have that, except (laughter) every once in a while you'll get a tape that (sigh) you play it back and it's so hard to understand. Even after you've checked it first. For some reason, the way the person talks, you understand it when they're talking to you, but when it's on the tape, some of the words just don't come out. There was some name that somebody used and I just couldn't get it. I must have played it back a thousand times, at a thousand speeds and finally did get it. But it was driving me nuts. Because it was real important to the story they were telling. Finally I figured out what they were saying.

Once in a while, there's a time when you've got to call them up and say, "What did you say when...?" And hope they would remember what we were talking about. (Laughter)

I really enjoy that. I've been to so many different places. Actually I concentrate on the Valley and the eastern counties of West Virginia, because so much of the overflow of settlement came from the Valley into the eastern counties of West Virginia.

Then, oddly enough, the western part of West Virginia was settled mostly from the Ohio Valley. So you get a lot of other ethnic groups that brought in their stories, but I wanted to interview people that had a relationship, whether it went back a hundred years or so, to see if the stories stayed the same or whether they had changed in the new area where they had gone.

It's really kind of funny sometimes the things that change. And the things that stay real close to the same. It's really, really interesting.

CD: Did you find a lot of that?
JLH: Kind of equal. A lot of the things, especially cures and things like that are pretty similar, but other things, like names of things, sometimes would have changed. A lot of times depending on what the ethnic background was, too. They'd have two different names for the cap on a shock of wheat. There'd be a different name just for the spread of the wheat on the top to get the moisture off of it. You'll find the same name used in one area, and then you go two more counties and it's different. And then you go to a farther county and it's the same as the one you started out in, so it's kind of following patterns of resettlement or something like that. It's interesting.

CD: And that's what you used to write the *Valley Folklife Series*?

JLH: First the folklore book.

CD: *Shenandoah Voices*?

JLH: Yes.

I'll tell you one of my biggest frustrations recently. I do this tour every fall called "The Valley Pike in War and Peace."

John told stories about people in words and wood. This one depicts Ben Southard in 1984.

More and more people are trying to get on it, but this last one that I did, there was this young woman and when she's getting off the bus after the tour, she said, "Oh Mr. Heatwole, thank you, I really enjoyed that. I'll never look at the Pike the same again." Then she said, "By the way, I've read some of your other books. I'm from Pendleton County, have you ever heard of a _?" She said this name, but of course there are all these other people getting off the bus too.

I said, "No, what's that?"

She said, "It's a thing that they made out of straw to keep witches away. Kind of a talisman."

I said, "Here's my card. Please call me tonight or tomorrow, whenever you can, because I want to talk to you about this more." I was trying to say goodbye to all these other people. And she never called me. I couldn't figure out who she was on the bus. It just drove me nuts. It's been a year. It's so frustrating. I think I've narrowed it down to who she is, but I keep calling the number and nobody answers. And there's no message machine or anything. That is really frustrating.

CD: Was it an outgrowth of the folklore that you became interested in the Civil War?

JLH: No. I was always interested in that too, even when I was a child. I remember the first Civil War books I had. I still have them over here. It's a four volume set. On the back of a comic book it said, "*Battles and Leaders of the Civil War*, Four Volume Set, $4.95."

I was real sick, I forget what I had, the flu or something. I felt I was near death, and my mother came in and said, "What can I do to make you feel better?" I said (whispers in sick voice), "Buy me *Battles and Leaders of the Civil War*."

It came in the mail. It was way too advanced for me at the time that I got them. I guess I was six or seven years old. (Laughter) But the pictures were great and I could read the captions on some of the things.

But that's what really got me interested because most of the stories in those four volumes were written by people who had actually participated. By reading it you felt a closer connection than say something that I might write. I haven't seen the war, I can only imagine what it must have been like. But it got me more interested in history that had some kind of direct attachment to somebody. You could put a face to the history, I think.

The real interest as far as the civilians came about because I realized that the Civil War wasn't fought on a bare pool table top. It was fought through villages and farms and people had their part in it too, directly or even indirectly.

This was one war where everybody in this country, except for some hermit somewhere, was somehow affected by it, and some in such horrible ways. The other part of it, people look at me really funny when I say it, but there are so many humorous stories too, that came out of it.

It's still so much a part of the lives of the people here in western Virginia. It permeates it.

I was interviewing a ninety-three-year-old man, I might have already told you this story, a couple of years ago, named Claude Rexrode and he lived in western Rockingham County. He had lived all ninety-three years right there beside Honey Run. When I'm interviewing him, I told him, "You know, I've interviewed probably close to a dozen people out in this area and they've all told me that same story about how Honey Run got its name, but I've never been able to tape anybody telling that story. Would you mind me taping you telling the story about how Honey Run got its name?" "Oh no, that's fine. I'll tell you how it got its name."

He was a real skinny little old man with a sunken chest. I turned on the tape recorder and he said, "Well, there was this young man and this young woman and they fell in love. Then the Civil War come along and they took him into the Confederate Army. One day she was walking along the creek and she knew he was camped a couple miles west of there with his fellow Confederates. She heard this shooting; Yankees were attacking that camp. She looked up the creek and she saw all these boys in gray running down the creek trying to get away from them Yankees. All of a sudden she saw her boyfriend and she yelled, 'Run, Honey, run!' And that's how Honey Run got its name."

I said, "What?" (Laughter)

He said, "Yep, that's how it got its name. Never heard any other story except that one." (Laughter)

CD: Was that not the story that you had heard?
JLH: No. The story that I had heard from almost twelve people was that a flood had come down the creek and had picked up some bee hives and of course dumped honey into the stream

and that's how it got the name, Honey Run. I told him that story and he said, "Nope. Never heard that. Never heard that one." Ninety-three years old. You figured he would have heard it from somebody, they all told me that. So I don't know whether there's two local legends or whether the rest of them were just pulling my leg. "Hey this guy might come over to talk to you. If he asks about Honey Run, tell him this one." But I just love that story. It's so much fun. There are just so many funny stories.

Millboro Springs in Bath County. There's a tombstone and chiseled on it is: "Here lies the father of twenty-nine. He would have had more but he didn't have time." (Laughter)

Twenty-nine. It's funny how those work in. I spoke last week in Roanoke for a Civil War roundtable. Before I spoke they introduced one of the members in the audience who is the grandson of a young Confederate courier, who had been a courier for Lee, and he was one of twenty-one children. So of course as soon as I got up, I said, "You know, that reminds me...." and I told about that tombstone.

There's two tombstones in Solomon Church Cemetery in southern Shenandoah County. Two sisters, (laughter) they're both carved and you see this carving everywhere, the hand pointing upward like this. Well, the one sister it's pointing up and the other it's pointing off to the side, like maybe she didn't go directly to heaven, she went somewhere else. (Laughter)

That's a lot of fun trying to find those kinds of things.

-Twelve-
The Gypsy Queen & Burk McCall

"Several bands of gypsies appeared in the Shenandoah Valley in the nineteenth-century, roving from Bath County in the south to Warren County in the north. These were the true Romany gypsies of Europe, descendants of tribes long settled in the British Isles....The gypsies of Rockingham were in the county by about 1850, with the last few members of the group moving away in the early 1930s....The Rockingham gypsies were from one of the three main tribes of English gypsies, the Stanleys. Their primary camp was near the hamlet of Lilly in the southwest quadrant of the county. It was described as a village of tents with stovepipes sticking out of them, both summer and winter. Some gypsies referred to houses as 'tents of stone.'"[14]

I remember my Uncle Paul, we used to ride around the countryside and go through cemeteries and he would tell stories about some of the people buried there. He used to always point out this one area along a fence at Ottobine Church in western Rockingham County. He said, "The Gypsy Queen is buried there; Dilly Stanley." And he would tell stories about the Gypsy Queen. Stories that his mother had told him.

Years later, I'm taking other people up there and they're saying, "How do you know she's buried there? There's nothing but these scrubby cedar bushes." I said, "Uncle Paul said it and

I believe him." He said that she was buried with her white horse.

Anyway, I was in the hospital in '91 and while I was in there they cleaned the cemetery out. And when they cleaned it out they found a little cement block with a half moon copper plaque on it that had her name on it.

Then I found, while I was finishing up the research for the first book, *Shenandoah Voices*, I found an undated obituary for her, saying Dilly Stanley died so and so, she was known as the Queen of the Gypsies for this part of the Shenandoah Valley. I got a call, maybe two months later, it was just kind of ironic how things happen, from a fellow in Maryland who was the president of the International Gypsy Folklore Society. He said, "Do you have any gypsy stories from your area?"

I told him some of the ones that I had and then I started to talk about Dilly Stanley.

He said, "That name's familiar. I think I have an obituary for her."

I said, "Oh, if you do, please, can you send me a copy of it? I've got it too, but I don't have the date."

He said, "Oh sure, I'll look it up. I'm pretty sure I've got it."

A few days later, a letter arrives and there's the obituary, but it's not the same one. It's a different one. It's got the date but it gives real specific details about how she died. She died of locked bowels, which is appendicitis. She was trying to get to another camp at Sangerville from her camp at Lilly, on Route 613. But she got too sick, right as they got to Beaver Creek below Ottobine Church, that's where she died. They said that she had a wagon that was full of beautiful brocades and really fancy. They burned all of that. They chloroformed her white horse, but they didn't bury the horse with her. They said they destroyed everything that she owned except for her two pet parrots. (Laughter) So there's this image of a gypsy with parrots on her shoulders.

That was another part of the story that I had never been able to fit together before. It even mentioned the name of two ministers that spoke at her service.

It's just uncanny sometimes where the information comes

from and how it comes. There are times where you get to a certain point in your research and you figure, I've done it all. There isn't going to be anything else, and there might not be anything for years, and then all of a sudden something that you looked for and just gave up on will just pop up, sometimes in the oddest places is where some of the materials come from.

Getting old like this now (laughter), it's really hard to remember some of the funny stories.

CD: I'm always amazed at how you remember the stories, the tidbits and things.

JLH: I remember some of them, but not all of them. Well, that's what they say about old people, right? They can remember things from when they were younger but can't remember to balance the checkbook, which is kinda like me. (Laughter)

Actually, this was one of the first stories that I ever heard, about the Gypsy Queen from Uncle Paul. After Lee surrendered at Appomattox, the Gypsy Queen supposedly showed up at my great-great grandmother, Elizabeth Heatwole's house, and she said, "Mrs. Heatwole, you have a red coverlet that I've admired for years." She would see it on her wash line when she'd walk by there. She said, "If you give me that coverlet, I'll tell your fortune."

My great-great grandmother was standing there smoking a corncob pipe and said, "Well, no, I don't believe in fortune telling. I'm not gonna do that."

The Gypsy Queen thought about it for another minute and said, "Tell you what I'll do. I'll tell your fortune anyway and if you think it's worthwhile, you can give me the coverlet." She said, "You've got two men off because of the war. Tonight they're both gonna come home. One'll come a walkin' and one'll come a ridin', one'll have money in his pockets and one'll have none."

Later that evening, my great-great grandfather, who had been a conscientious objector, but had served a year in the war, figuring they'd leave him alone, but instead they drafted him for three more years. After he'd served that first year, he'd gone back into the mountains of what became West Virginia and he was working in apple orchards and so when he came walking over the mountains he had money in his pockets.

Later that night, Elizabeth's brother-in-law, who was married to her younger sister, Frank Murray was his name, he was a Confederate cavalryman, and he came riding back from Appomattox on an old bony horse and didn't have a penny to his name.

So everybody always says, "Did she get the coverlet?"

We don't know. It's a terrible letdown at the end of the story but it gives it more credence, because we don't know whether she got it or not. But that was a great story. The first time I heard it, the hair just kind of rose up on the back of my neck.

Frank Murray and my great-great grandfather, are both buried in the same cemetery, Bank Church Cemetery. It's just one of those things, you just love tracing those stories and then you hear other stories about the same people from other families in the area.

One woman that I interviewed from Clover Hill said that her mother, when she was eight or ten years old, had heard about the Gypsy Queen being ill down by Beaver Creek. She and a friend of hers picked some flowers and went down there and gave them to her before she died. Handed her these bouquets of flowers. That was kind of interesting.

They were very typical of what you would see as gypsies, their way of life. They would go through the countryside, mend pots and pans, things like that. Every spring, down along Muddy Creek, they would strip pussy willows and they'd make baskets and they would sell those. I've seen one of those baskets. That's how they made ends meet, either as farm hands during harvest season, they would hire out for those kinds of things, but mostly mending the pots and pans and making these baskets that they would sell from door to door.

The band was about seventy-five, eighty people. Of course after she died, it just kind of dwindled down until there was only a few left. The last one supposedly left in the 1930s and moved somewhere up north, Pennsylvania or New York.

I remember that probably in the late 1970s, early 1980s, a

bunch of gypsies came back here and they rented Natural Chimneys Park and they were there for a week. Supposedly a lot of them were descendants of hers.

I asked somebody, "Let's go back there and talk to them." He said, "They won't tell you the truth about any of it. They'll probably just clam up or either just tell you a bunch of lies." I should've gone back anyway and tried to do it.

CD: Are there still bands of gypsies around?
JLH: No, I don't think like back then. Back then they would actually have a camp for each season that they would go to. I've had people describe what the camps looked like. These wagons or tents with stovepipes coming out of them in the winter time.

There were several different bands. The one that was at Sangerville is kind of interesting too because I think I'm the first one to separate one story.

One story was that Dilly Stanley was married to a man named Burk McCall, a Scots-Irishman and that he had abducted her from the band and married her and then the gypsies caught up with them and took him into the band. He was supposed to be a stock trader from the Sangerville area, very successful. It was always linked, the Gypsy Queen and Burk McCall.

Turns out that they weren't linked. They might have known each other, but he actually was at a horse trading fair over in Moorefield, West Virginia, there were always gypsies at the horse trading things, and he met a young gypsy princess, we don't know what her first name was, her last name was Harrison. Apparently for those couple of days, they fell in love and she said, "My people will never accept you." He said, "Well, let's just go away and they'll have to. We'll get married."

He knew horses so well that they started riding, galloping back towards Augusta County and every time that he knew that the horses were going to show signs of giving out or playing out, he would stop and trade them for fresh horses. So they got back to Augusta County, two or three days before the gypsies

The grave marker of Dilly, the Gypsy Queen.

could catch up with them. Got married and when they got here they just took up residence. I think I was the first one to find out that the old story wasn't quite true.

I've interviewed a lot of people that knew Burk McCall. This is back in the 70s when there were still a lot of people living that had been born in the 1880s. They would tell stories about him as an old man and how feisty he was.

One of the stories was that late one night he was walking along a road and some guy came by in a buggy and they stopped and talked for a few minutes. Burk McCall said to this guy, "Have you ever heard of Burk McCall?" The guy in the buggy said, "Yeah, I hear that he's a no good scoundrel that will cheat you at the drop of a hat." Burk McCall said, "Well, I'm that no good scoundrel," and pulled him down off of the buggy and beat him up. (Laughter) Something like a seventy-year-old man beating up this guy. It's funny.

Those stories are kind of interesting because they overlap counties. Whereas a lot of the stories, they are very mated to the areas that you're doing the research in but every once in a while you'll find one that links up.

-Thirteen-
Civil
War

"To this day, when Valley natives mention 'The War,' they don't mean anything but the Civil War; it is just understood."[15]

In the Civil War, General Custer, after the Battle of Fisher's Hill, was still commanding a brigade of cavalry. He had been given, like all the other cavalry commanders, orders by General Sheridan that if they caught anybody in civilian clothes with a rifle they were supposed to execute them as bushwhackers.

The legend has always been in Rockingham County and Shenandoah County that he picked up this young man, Davy Getz with a squirrel rifle, tied a rope around his neck and tied him to the back of his headquarters' wagon and brought him further up the Valley, south in the Valley. The story was always that he was this young man. When I started doing the research, I found out that he was thirty-nine. He wasn't a teenager, nineteen or twenty, but they said he had a mind of a six-year-old.

This is an odd occurrence, because right after the book [*The Burning*] came out, I don't know why I was doing it, I was looking for some other photograph over at the Historical Society in Dayton. I started going through this album and they were all Shenandoah County people and one of them was Adolf Heller.

Adolf Heller. When Custer first caught Davy Getz and

started to leave the Woodstock area where he had captured him, the town fathers, some of the leading men of the town, were following and one of them was Adolf Heller. He was about in his sixties and he was a storekeeper in the town. He was pleading with Custer, "Please don't hurt him. Please don't take him away. He didn't mean anything. He has the mind of a child." Custer just ignored him. Finally Adolf Heller said to Custer, "You will sleep in a bloody grave for this." Of course he did in 1876 out on the Little Big Horn.

The story of Davy Getz, I was able to expand it a lot. First getting his age right. When I looked him up in the 1860 census records, they show his mother and father who were in their seventies. They list the father as a farmer, they list the mother as a housekeeper, then comes Davy and he's not listed as anything, and then comes his younger brother who's listed as farm hand. So I think that points towards maybe he wasn't that functional.

The other thing was that when the war broke out his brother joined the Seventh Virginia Cavalry. For somebody with a feeble mind like Davy, you have to think that he probably worshipped that younger brother, "My brother the soldier, he's out there with his gun." I think that's what happened with Davy. Who else would let their child or old person go out with a gun when there're thousands of troops coming through? He picked it up and went out because he wanted to play soldier and he ended up dying for it.

The rest of the story was that he was executed just south of Dayton on the Joseph Coffman property. When I was doing the research, I found a letter written by Elizabeth Coffman, who was eighteen years old and she was the granddaughter of the people that owned that property where he was executed. The letter was written ten days after the Union Soldiers had left Rockingham County. She was writing to a cousin of hers who was in the Confederate cavalry. She wrote, "A couple of days after the Yankees got

Courtesy Shenandoah Valley Battlefields Foundation

John Heatwole, the Civil War teacher, shares his knowledge of the war while standing in the shadow of the Prayer Tree in northern Augusta County. Legend says that the ancient oak tree marked the site where Confederate General Thomas Jonathan "Stonewall" Jackson conducted religious services.

here, they took one of our men out in the orchard, made him dig his own grave and shot him." Of course, part of the legend was that he had been made to dig his own grave.

Then I found a story in another family, the Thompson family. Young Andy Thompson was thirteen years old when this happened. His mother was a widow and had all these younger children, so he was hiring himself out to different farmers to do odd jobs. When Lieutenant John Rogers Meigs was killed in a fire fight with Confederate scouts on the evening of October 3, 1864, Andy had been working for the people that had the closest house to that spot and of course Sheridan ordered all the houses burned in that area. Noah Wenger and his family left the house, they knew it was gonna be burned down. Andy stayed and when they came and started setting fires, he took a crock off a fence post, they used to put broken or chipped crocks on fence posts to keep them from rotting, and got water from somewhere and he kept dousing the fires that they were setting. Finally the soldiers just said, the heck with it. Let the kid have the place. When the Wengers came back, their house was still there. It's kind of interesting.

To tie it in to the Davy Getz episode. When Davy Getz was executed they say he fell back into the grave but his feet were sticking out. They just left him there, they didn't fill in the grave. Another thirteen-year-old named Zume Brown, who was a friend of this Thompson boy, came to the house and said, "You know that man they shot up in Coffman's orchard? He has a brand new pair of boots on. Let's go get them."

They went up there and the Thompson boy supposedly put his arms under Davy Getz's arms while Zume Brown tried to get the boots off and when they moved him, gas or something escaped from his throat and he gurgled. That scared them to death and they ran off. But the next morning, Thompson was working around the farm and Zume

Brown walked by and he had the boots on. He said, "I went back and got them. I figured he'd be dead by now."

This little story turned into a much longer story. Zume Brown, when he was twenty years old, was at the county fair here in Augusta County and some trustee from the insane asylum stabbed him to death. No reason, just stabbed him to death. Strange stories.

John knew that cemeteries held stories about the Civil War and about everyday life from times gone by. This wooden grave marker was discovered by him in his travels.

-Fourteen-
Witchery

"My great-uncle Paul rather matter-of-factly re-lated that in his youth (around the year 1900), witches and their hexes were quite common. His attitude was that the witches were considered a nuisance for the most part and that if you avoided crossing them they were harmless. On the other hand, my uncle had at one time known a sorcerer, a male witch, and his opinion of this man was radi-cally different from the one he held about the women who dabbled in black magic. Sorcerers were considered truly evil and dangerous; he was reluc-tant to mention the sorcerer's name even though the man had been dead for seventy years."[16]

I think with all the interviews, the thing that has surprised me the most is the number of witch stories.

There are so many. Today when I get book lists, there's always a new book about the Salem witch trials. Over and over and over again as if it didn't happen anywhere else. The other thing that I collect are books from other states on their folklore and there's very little witch lore. They must have had witch lore because all of them came from the British Isles or Germany or Northern Ireland where there were rich traditions in that.

When you talk to people here, I'll talk to people on a park bench or at a bench out at the mall and I'll ask, "Did you grow up here?" "Yeah, I grew up here." "Ever hear any witch stories?" "Well, yeah, I don't know whether I want to talk about them." There's so many of them. It's unbelievable. I must have a couple hundred witch stories. Very specific things too.

The only local historians that really ever wrote about them, Elmer Smith and John Stewart and Ellsworth Kyger, wrote about them when they did the book, *Shenandoah Valley Folklore* for the Pennsylvania Folklore Society.

The only earlier book was Peyton's *History of Augusta County* and he talks about a few of the traditions, not many, but a few of them. When you go interview people, it's just uncanny how many of them can be traced back to the British Isles or to Germany where similar things happened.

Like collecting urine. If your baby has been hexed and just cries all the time, you get the urine in a bottle, cork it up and either put it inside the fireplace or hang it up inside the chimney. For some reason they thought that caused strangury in the witches where they wouldn't be able to urinate and they'd have to come back to the house and release the hex on the baby in order to have relief themselves. There're a lot of stories around here about that.

Probably the most detailed one is from the hollow that the Orkney Grade goes through in western Shenandoah County. There was this boy who supposedly had just bedeviled this old woman so much that she put a curse on him where he couldn't urinate. He was in terrible agony and his people kept asking, "What have you done lately that might have caused this?"

Finally he said, "That old woman who lives up that path there, I was throwing rocks at her, and she said she was gonna curse me."

The family members and some of their neighbors, kind of like out of a movie with pitchforks and torches, go up the road to confront the woman. When she saw them coming, they were just getting into her yard, she started to run. Some of them peeled off and started chasing her but when the others got up on her porch, there was an animal bladder full of something and somebody picked up a stick and hit it, and all this urine gushed out. Right at that point, the boy released too. The front of his trousers were all wet.

Just real specific things like that.

I've even had family members tell me stories on their own ancestors who were supposedly witches. Some of them not very complimentary. I've actually gone to some of these places and seen the sites and found their gravesites.

In some of the witch stories that I've heard, I've had some descriptions of some of these people. I've actually found photographs of two of them who were supposedly witches, which I probably could never use because they have family still around. (Laughter)

I think in doing the folklore and folklife interviews, that's the hardest part. Some of the stories are just really wonderful but you have to draw a line somewhere and you ask the people, "Look, can we use the name?" If they say, "Well, I'd rather not." I say, "How about the story without the name?" A lot of times they'll say, "Yeah, do that. But don't use the name." I always make a note, <u>do not use name in the story</u>.

There was one woman, just passed away, she was one hundred and one. She told me some really great stories and most of them, she'd said, "Yeah, you can go ahead and use them," but there were some others that she didn't want her name used. Her son just said, "Ma was just worried that somebody would come back to her on it. You can go ahead and tell any of the stories you want to." She was a neat lady from over in Grottoes.

People really did believe in it. I think a lot of the people that supposedly were witches were doing it because they knew they could bend people to their wills. Who's gonna refuse a witch a cup of sugar or flour? (Laughter) Man, give it to her, don't want to cross her.

CD: Weren't witches also the healers or the herb doctors?
JLH: There are a few of the people that I've talked to that told witch stories who have also talked about some of those witches actually being herb doctors too, or even midwives that could cure.

In the research that I've done, I found out that basically it

Courtesy JMU Special Collections

**Wispy spirits of "haints" (ghosts)
appeared in one of John's sketches**

was the church. Back during the middle ages, or even the dark ages maybe, that they wanted people to rely more on them than relying on these, what they called back then, wise women, who knew about different concoctions and poultices. So they put this onerous label on them, "Oh no, they're in league with the devil." And eventually that they're witches.

I really do think that there were people who thought that they could do these things. There're just as many, if not more, who could cure, they had their specialties, goiters or warts, even some that said they could cure cancer.

There's a really wonderful story here in Augusta County, it took place back on the road to Craigsville. There was a woman back there who had just terrible outbreaks of cancer on her arm and a really famous doctor from Staunton went to see her. His name was Waddell. He looked at it and said, "Yes. You've got a cancer. We're gonna have to get you into town sometime in the next week and we're gonna have to operate and see if we can take that off."

A couple of days passed and he came back to Staunton and she's making plans to come in to have this operation. This old man came walking up the road from the direction of Williamsville and stopped to talk to one of her neighbors. One of the neighbors told him about this woman on the next farm down having this terrible cancer and he said, "Take me to her."

They go to her and he looks at it and he said, "If you'll trust me, I can get rid of that." She said, "What have I got to lose? Okay, what do you want to do?" He said, "I'm gonna do some things. I don't want anybody to speak. It's not gonna hurt you but nobody can speak while I do this or even after I do it. Nobody can talk to me while I leave." She said, "Okay."

He took out an old, dirty handkerchief and he started brushing it across her arm where this cancer was and mumbling something under his breath. Then he asked her for a couple of coins and he put them in the handkerchief and tied it into a knot. Then he went outside and he picked up a shovel that was leaning up against the house and took this handkerchief over to this apple tree and dug a hole and buried the handkerchief and the coins in the hole. Then he left and he didn't say another word.

Within a day the cancer started clearing up. A few days later when she was supposed to go see the doctor, it was almost all the way gone. She went in to Staunton anyway and he looked at it and he said, "I don't know what's going on here but it's looking a lot better. Let's just leave it alone and see if it comes back again."

Within about a week it was totally gone. Her skin was blemish free. They said that summer the tree got apples on it, but they never grew any bigger than the end of your thumb. By the fall they just all turned black and fell off the tree. It would always bear but the apples would never become mature, they would always wither away and fall off the tree.

Supposed to be a true story. People believed all of that. Like I said, there were supposed to be healers that had just certain specialties, things they could do.

The wart cures, there's just hundreds and hundreds and hundreds of those. Some of those can be traced back pretty far, especially here in Augusta County. In some of the early letters people talk about some of the cures that they would use for getting rid of the warts.

It's easy to see where somebody who had that kind of power would be suspected of having even worse kinds of powers. The black powers, something like that.

In 1898, they held the annual conference for the Dunkers in Sangerville. What they do at these annual conferences is people would put questions to them about how they should lead their lives. One of the questions that was put to the elders of the church was: "Should a member of the congregation be a witch doctor?" Witch doctors were the ones who could take hexes off. They answered, "No, we don't think that people who practice breaking hexes should be communicants with the church." It's too close to being an actual witch, maybe is what they were thinking. I thought it was interesting that that came down through the church records, that at that time there were still a lot of witch doctors around who could break these hexes.

Talking about witches, I've got names of maybe twenty female witches and only have names of one or two male witches, because they were supposed to be much more powerful and much more evil. Even my great uncle who was close to ninety when he passed away, he said he knew a wizard. He wouldn't even name his name, even though this guy had been dead for seventy years. He felt too much horror in even thinking about the power that this fellow had. So he wouldn't even mention his name even though he'd been dead all that time.

In some areas they would call them wizards and then in the Brocks Gap area, you've probably run into them calling them warlocks. It depends on the area. Some of the things that they could do and the ways to break those hexes are fairly common throughout the region.

One of the witches that I've done some research on was from back in Brocks Gap. This witch, the stories are just very specific. Pretty interesting. I know that one of her descendants wasn't too happy that I was collecting these stories. (Laughter) She said, "I don't know where this comes from but my granny was a wonderful, church going woman. She never would have done any of this." That's what's really odd because I've actually spoken to other descendants of the same woman and they say, "Oh yea. Granny was a witch." So I guess it all depends on your perspective.

The interesting thing about it is, unlike the Salem witch trials, these people were actually members of the community. If they didn't do something too horrendous, they were just kind of accepted that they were people who had special powers. You just kind of walked on your tiptoes around them. You definitely didn't want to get in trouble by insulting them in any way.

The littlest things could really turn them against you, to have them try to do something to plant a seed in your mind that you were going to get sick or die.

There was a witch, and I think I've identified her, who lived on Little North Mountain. She and her husband only had one horse, or one mule, and they would ride down to Fulks Run. One time, and this story was told to me by a woman who as a child was there when it happened, she said they were playing outside of the Fulks Run Store and this woman and her husband came riding down. One boy, a little bit older that was all the time getting into trouble, started throwing dirt clods at them. She looked at him and said, "Boy, if I had your picture I could do something to you you wouldn't be very happy about."

If witches could get your picture, they could put some real hurtin' on you. This woman said, "We just stood there with our

mouths open. He never threw another dirt clod at them again."
He was scared to death when she said that.

There's a man who lives here in Staunton, he's way up
there in age right now, who grew up in Brocks Gap. He said
that there was a witch that lived on one of those little mountains back in there. He said that he often heard this old man
say, "If I could just get a piece of her clothing, I could get rid of
her, in a hurry." There are all these witch doctor stories.

The funny thing about it is when you hear the stories, when
you collect them, if it's a full story with a beginning and a middle
and an end, the end is usually the witch getting her comeup-
pance. They're almost little morality plays. You never hear of
the witch actually coming out on top.

The only one where the witch came out on top is the one

Courtesy Bruce Rossenwasser

**John's carvings, like this
1996 wooden box, often
had an air of mystery
and the supernatural.**

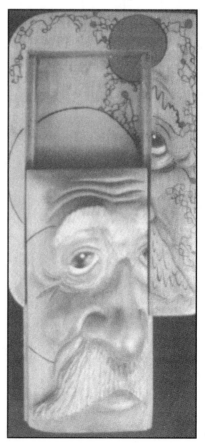

about the young woman who had hexed people's cattle, and she just had a bad temper. She would do things like that; hex their cattle, or their guns or their babies.

Then she fell in love with this young man and he fell in love with her. He said, "Look, I want to marry you, but I can't marry you unless you promise me as long as we're together that you won't practice witchcraft." She said, "All right. I love you, too. I won't practice witchcraft."

He died in 1939 and of course the tradition of the time was that the body would be kept at the house for a couple of days. People would come and keep vigil with the widow, more than anything else to make sure that they weren't in some kind of a deep coma that they were going to come out of after you buried them.

It was the turn of these three little girls who were all around ten years old, and they were sent down to this log cabin. There was a fire going and they sat on stools in front of this old lady, who everybody had heard stories about, that she had been a witch when she was younger. The old lady is sitting there rocking, back and forth, back and forth, smoking a pipe, rocking back and forth.

All of a sudden she stops, and "creak," stops rocking, and leans forward and takes the pipe out of her mouth and looks at these three little girls, whose eyes are already as big as saucers and says, "Well, now that Pap's gone, I guess I'll have to go back to witchin'."

They just popped up and ran out of the room as fast as they could, back to their homes. Those three women are still alive. I interviewed each one of them separately and they all told the same story, that that really did happen. Great, great, story.

There's one artifact I'll show you before you go. I have an artifact that comes from Browns Cove which is on the east side of Browns Gap in Southeastern Rockingham County and it was in a community of blacks. It's a voodoo doll or a "hoodoo doll" as they call it. It is so spooky. It's made out of a wishbone of a chicken or a turkey, and they've dipped the head in tar and the little feet in tar and they've put little red eyes and mouth on it. But then they've made this little dress or skirt with it, when you open it up there are all these pins inside of it. I don't know the story behind that, except that the cape is red. Red is supposed to signify, not so much a hex, but a charm, to bring your lover to you.

That's the only thing I found except for one other thing when they were tearing down a really old drover's tavern in Bridgewater, they found a child's shoe in the wall. Reading in witch lore, that supposedly is a good talisman to keep witches out of your house, to put a child's shoe in the wall when you're building it. I'll show that to you too. It's really early, it's not a right or a left shoe, it's one of the ones that's cut from one pattern and you wear it long enough and it forms to your foot. It just looked like a piece of old dirty rag or something. I put Neat's foot oil in it and kept pushing stuff in it to form it, and tying it up. Now it looks pretty good. Yeah.

What I really want is one of those little bottles of urine. Peyton wrote the history of Augusta County, and he wrote that in the late 1800s. And he said that when they were tearing down an old house in Staunton they found one of those up in the chimney. It was one of his few things that he talked about with the witch lore.

The only thing that I haven't done, and I don't know if I ever will, but I haven't tried to pin any body down that still thought they could do the witchcraft. I don't know if anybody's still doing that. Everybody I talk to doesn't believe it, but they've got those specific stories, so who knows?

-Fifteen-
High Words
& Magic Cures

"Granny women and herb doctors could help out during childbirth and would treat most afflictions not involving surgery. When one of these people felt a case was beyond his or her ability to effect a cure there were powerful options to be considered: magic cures and incantations."[17]

I know there are people that know the herb lore and there still are people doing what I call magic cures, most of them using something from the Bible. Some of them, seem like they come from way, way back in time.

I've also collected stories about the people that could stop blood with the high words.

I could never find the high words until one day I was interviewing a woman from back over in Hopkins Gap. She said, "When I was little, we were playing out in the garden. I was about five years old and I tripped, and when I fell, I cut my leg open on a piece of glass, and the blood was just spurting out. Somebody called for my daddy and he came running and picked me up and put his hand across my little calf. The blood was just spurting through his fingers and then he said the high words. As soon as he said the high words, the blood stopped like that." She snapped her fingers.

I asked, "Well, do you know what the high words were?"

She said, "No, but it was Ezekiel 16:6 from the Bible." That's: "And when I passed thee, and saw thee polluted in thine own blood, I said unto thee when thou wast in thy blood, Live; yea, I said unto thee when thou wast in thy blood, Live."

Most of the people that I've interviewed that knew that it came from the Bible said that that's what it was, but there have been a few other people who've said that "no," it was something else. So there might be some other ones but that's the main one.

The reason I told you the blood stopping story was because it may be something in their physiology, when somebody tells them they can stop it, they stop it themselves.

Back in Highland County, I interviewed a woman and she said, "We had a visit from Sis Gum who was supposed to be the witch in our area, but she also did other things. She could do cures and magic cures. We had a horse that had somehow broken part of a fence and there was a nail sticking out and it had gouged its hindquarters, a big place, blood was flowing from it like crazy. My father said, 'Can you help us out? Will you stop the blood on the horse?' She said, 'Oh, people just won't leave me alone. Okay, I'll go do it.' She went out and didn't touch the horse at all but stood beside it and mumbled some words and the blood stopped."

So my question, the first time I heard that, I thought, "Did that horse believe?" It's uncanny because all the people that I have interviewed that have had blood stopped, and there's quite a few still living, they all swear by it. A lot of times they don't know the words but they knew the person came and stopped it.

There was a woman who lived in Bridgewater and I'd heard that she could stop blood. I called her up on the phone and I said, "Is it true that you can stop blood?"

She said, "Yeah. I haven't done it for about fifty years, but I used to do it all the time."

I said, "So somebody would get a bloody nose or something that wouldn't stop bleeding or a wound that wouldn't stop bleeding and you'd go over to their house and say the words?"

She said, "No, I'd do it over the phone." (Laughter)

That's a new one. Remote control stopping blood. She used Ezekiel 16:6 too.

This links in to herb cures too. One fellow that I interviewed said that when he was little, he went running in the kitchen one day and his mother was just taking a pot of boiling water off the stove and was turning, he ran right into her and it scalded him all down his front. He said the mother and the grandmother took him into the bedroom and ripped his shirt off. The grandmother, she chewed tobacco, started spitting tobacco juice and rubbing it down his front. He said, "I was screaming. The pain was unbearable." Then after she did that, she did her hand in the air over the area and started mumbling something under her breath, and he said, "Then it stopped, no pain."

Now the tobacco juice helped. Because it kind of cauterized the nerve endings I guess. But you know something that horrible, that's not going to do it all. He said he never had a blister.

There have been a lot of people that have told me the same thing for the stopping of the blood or for the pain like that.

There's a woman named, I shouldn't name her name..., because I can't remember it, that's why. (Laughter) She lives over near Harriston, here in Augusta County, and I had heard that she takes the fire out of burns. I asked her about that and she wouldn't tell me the things she uses. She said, "I've helped a couple hundred people probably in my life that have had bad burns. You know, I think really they have to believe. If they don't believe, it's not going to work. That's the only way it'll work." So who knows?

Now for taking the pain out of a burn, there are maybe four different ones that I've been able to collect for that. One is something about a new moon, which has nothing to do with the Bible, but all the rest of them, it either has to do with the Bible, or it has to do with religion. One of the things I found to take fire out of, or the pain out of burns is: "Three angels came from the east, one bearing frost, and one bearing fire. And I said, In frost, out fire." And the pain was gone. "In the name of the Father and the Son and the Holy Spirit." They say that three times. The angels are in there, so they're still trying to tie it back to religion.

There was another woman, who's dead now, that lived near Penn Laird. She was a wart doctor and could take away warts using different rituals. She said, "I had nieces and nephews that

**"Cure to take out Fire" found on the back
of a Civil War era document from
Rockingham County.**

always said I was a witch woman because I could take these warts off." That was the other thing that people swore by.

I have a story about Ken Schuler's daughter.

First, my great-aunt who was from Frederick County, Virginia, she said when she was a little girl if you got warts you rub a stick on each of your warts, then you tie it up in real pretty paper and tie a bow around it. Then you leave it on a path that other children travel and whoever picks up this pretty package and opens it up, they get your warts, right? She said, "Oh, that worked. That really worked."

So Keena, Ken's daughter, had warts all over her hand, and this was right before she left for the summer to go out to Colorado where she'd gotten a scholarship to run track.

I said, "Keena, let me tell you, my great-aunt had a way of getting rid of warts. Why don't you try it? It might work for you."

She said, "What is it?"

I said, "Go get a stick. Rub it on each of your warts, tie

pretty paper around it, tie a bow around it and leave it outside of the locker of somebody you don't like at school." There was only a week of school left.

She said, "Okay, I'll do it."

I saw her just before she left and she's got her hands on her hips and she says, "I did that, and I left it outside the locker of this girl that I can't stand. I've still got the warts."

It's a week later and I said, "You've got to be patient. You've gotta believe in it."

She said, "I don't believe in it because it should've been done by now." So she leaves for school.

The other thing I didn't tell you was that Keena had had operations on them, had had them frozen, had had them cut. Anything you could think of, and it had never worked, they had always come back.

Courtesy Ken Schuler

John Heatwole with Keena Schuler (and her bunny).

Anyway, I see her at Thanksgiving and she says, "Guess what? Guess what? The end of the first week when I was out in Colorado, they went away." They still haven't come back. That was ten years ago, now.

So who knows? (Laughter) I was just kind of kidding around, but it worked, it actually worked on her. There are so many.

Some people say, well you've gotta rub a warm chicken's foot on it and then bury it in the side of a hill and that will get rid of your warts.

Others say, nope, skin off a chicken's gizzard, that's what you rub on it and bury under the drip of a roof or something.

One guy back in West Virginia told me about a bedeviled pencil, which was a pencil with purple lead that this witch doctor, or wart doctor, would just lick the end of it and he'd put a dot on each of your warts and they would go away within a week.

These people all swear. This one fellow that I interviewed back in Clover Hill, said that his father told him that when he was a boy that he had warts just everywhere on his hands. Big ugly mounds of warts and that he went back to some guy over near Singers Glen who "witched them off." He didn't know how he did it, but "witched them off," and they all went away.

Jim Swope told the story that if you have warts, you prick them with a pin til they bleed a little bit and then take a kernel of corn and dab it in it and feed it to a hen and your warts will go away.

Back at Clover Hill one time I was speaking to the Ruritans there and I told that. After my talk was over this man came up and said, "You know that story about the kernel of corn was pretty interesting but it's wrong."

I said, "What do you mean it's wrong?"

He says, "You do it just the way you said but you've got to feed it to a rooster for it to go away." (Laughter)

So in that area it was the rooster, the other area it was the hen. Whatever works for you, I guess is okay.

There are just so many different cures. As I said, most of them, except for the wart cures, and even a few wart cures, have had little incantations that I haven't been able to find that people said they mumbled. Most of them don't have incantations, it's just the ritual. So many of them talk about this mumbled incantation. If anybody else hears it, it gets diluted. So you hold it very close to your vest, or keep it in your family.

CD: It's fascinating how your work, you being involved with it for so many years, it's all tying together and people come to you with the stories.

JLH: I just can't keep my mouth shut. Especially when I'm talking to an older person. I always ask, "Did you grow up here?"

I've talked to other people too that didn't grow up here

and I wish they had. One guy from Georgia was staying up at Massanutten and I did a program up there one night. He said, "Back in Georgia there was this witch doctor. What he did didn't really involve people that much."

I asked, "What do you mean?"

He said that there was this little old house that belonged to a widow and it had trees around it where a lot of the limbs had gone dead. It was very dangerous, that these could come off and destroy this old woman's house, she wouldn't have anywhere to go. This guy came by one day and she was talking about that, how she was worried about the house because of these limbs being right over it. He said, "Don't you worry about it. You just go to bed and I'll take care of it." Somebody else was with him and he took out two ears of corn from inside his coat and he banged them together and said, "Okay, everything's gonna be all right." Then he left. They never saw him again. The next morning all those limbs were down, none of them had touched the house. They had broken off, they hadn't been sawed off. Kind of weird.

He said this witch doctor could summon lightning or thunder with the ears of corn.

I also think for many years that people outside this area thought that, well not just this area, but other areas of Appalachia, they thought that the people were backwards. But I think the thing is that the people stayed at home and their descendants stayed at home. Whereas where these other people are coming from it's been very homogenized so they don't hear these kinds of things.

They get over here and they think, well, these people are really behind the times. And it's not that at all, it's just that it's died out in the other areas. Or the memory of it.

Brocks Gap, one of the first people that I ever talked to back there was a Turner woman and I don't even remember who she was. There was always a tradition back there of people being descended from Indian women. She said, "I know my husband is. He'll go out in the morning to start his farm chores, but first he sniffs the air, and if he smells game he calls his dog and I don't see him again for the rest of the day." She said, "He's got Indian blood in him."

-Sixteen-
Kris Kringling
& Belsnickling

"Belsnickling is the most common term used to describe the custom of dressing in a disguise and having people in the neighborhood try to guess your identity as you and your friends, or family members, walk from house to house...the only difference between belsnickling and kris kringling is the name."[18]

This is kind of uncanny too, this really is. I bought a photograph that was made by D.H. Hill at Bridgewater and he traveled all throughout the areas. I guess he had put the name on the back, "Cam Strawderman and wife." They were from back on the border between Brocks Gap and Hardy County. He's sitting in a straight chair with a log cabin behind him, and she's standing behind with her hand on his shoulder, and if she isn't an Indian, I don't know what she is. She looks like she just came out of a John Wayne movie. To make a long story short, I found this photograph years and years ago.

The year before last, I went kris kringling with a group from back around Mathias. They had somebody else call ahead to people and say, "We've got a group that's coming out kris kringling, would you care if they came by your house?" Because they didn't want to get shot. (Laughter)

I was dressed as a huge, lady rabbit, I had a long green dress on. In fact, my mask is over in that box there. I made it out of a pillow case, and I just tied up the corners like ears and then drew the rabbit face on it.

We must have gone to half a dozen or more places. I'll tell you about one of the places and then I'll tell you what I'm leading up to. One of the places we went to was on the side of a mountain. The place was so weather-beaten, it looked like it wasn't going to stand up for another minute, but they had a satellite dish out there. We went inside, here are all these barefoot kids, this is December 28th of 2002. We go in and these kids, their eyes are huge. Everybody's sitting around on chairs with the stuffing coming out of them. And the cracks, the ceiling's coming down. They were watching the Beverly Hillbillies on television. (Laughter)

Anyway, we went to another house and we went in and all over the walls were bear heads and skins and deer antlers. They introduced me to this guy and his last name was Strawderman. I asked, "Do you have an ancestor named Cam?"

He said, "Yes, he was a blacksmith back here."

I said, "What was he to you?"

He said, "He was my great grandfather."

I asked, "What did you know about your great grandmother?"

He answers, "Not really anything."

I said, "Did you know she was an Indian?"

He said, "Was she really?"

I said, "I've got a photograph of him with her standing behind him." This guy's real dark, I mean he looked like an Indian.

His wife said, "I knew he was an Indian. He'd rather be in the woods than anywhere." (Laughter) It was so funny. So I sent him a copy of the photograph.

It's just funny how things come together. I never knew that Cam Strawderman was a blacksmith so I got another little piece of the story too.

The kris kringling, that's what they call it back there. You get more into Brocks Gap and over into this area and it becomes belsnickling. I know now what all the fun was about because it was fun. Nobody knew me from Adam except the people I was with, but I was changing my voice and everybody was trying to guess who I was. This one old lady, I've got a photograph of her feeling my arms, because everything was covered, our hands and everything, trying to look in my eyes to see who I was, and of course she didn't know me.

At one house, they couldn't guess me, and people were getting frustrated and one of the people I was with said, "Use your real voice." So I used my real voice and this woman said, "That's the guy from the radio! What's his name? John Something."

So I got guessed at one place. It was so much fun. One woman who was with us, she had left the area, she had moved to Harrisonburg and she hadn't been back in twenty or thirty years. She had this old guy in this one house, she went and sat on his lap. She's going, "You know who I am, don't you?" He's trying to look in her eyes and is feeling her arms, "Oh, you know who I am!" Then she started giving him little hints and finally he goes, "Damn it, you aren't Marcie So and So." She says, "Yes, I am." She pulled off her mask and he hadn't seen her for thirty years. They both started crying.

They went out this last December, and I couldn't go with them. I think there are some pictures up there on the desk that they sent me. One of the costumes this year was a riot. It's some kind of monster. When I went, I was the big lady rabbit. There was a Mrs. Santa Claus. It was so cold that every time we went into someplace we got all heated up and then back out into the cold and her breath in the mask started making things run and she looked like Frankenstein's wife at the end of the thing. Some just dressed like bums, but oh, it was so much fun. They want to try to do it at least every two or three years. We met at one house and all of us put on our costumes.

All that kind of died out around World War II because people were afraid of saboteurs. I'm sure that Nazis are going to show up at your house in costume, to take over, run their cell from your cabin somewhere. But people were worried about that, so they stopped doing it.

I'm not sure where my pictures are, but the pictures are really funny because I'm sitting there, I look real coy, and the woman's feeling my arm. She's about eighty years old, feeling my arm. I'm saying, "You'll never guess." "Yes, I will!" "No you won't."

I think I'm the first person to link the bel-snickling to shang-hai-ing. Especially along the border between Augusta and Rockingham, because you have Scots-Irish mostly on one side and the Germans on the other. I just felt because of what I could find out

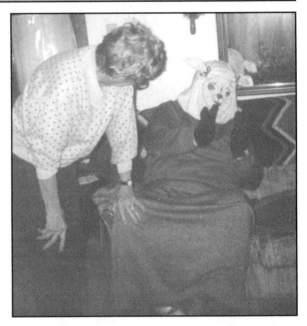

John in his "bunny rabbit" kris kringling costume, December 28, 2002.

about shanghai-ing, that it came later, and then it kind of got mixed up on the border, some people called shanghai-ing, belsnickling and vice-versa. In shanghai-ing, they'd get up in these really fancy kind of costumes and on Christmas day they'd parade through the villages and through Staunton and make noise and make a racket. In fact, in Scots-Irish, or I guess it's Gaelic, "Coli-shangi" means raising a ruckus. I think they did it because they were jealous of the Germans doing belsnickling. They wanted to do something like that too.

That's the only place you found shanghai-ing was in the Scots-Irish areas, but along the border, like I said, in Rockingham and in Augusta they kind of intertwined or inter-mixed the two titles.

In some areas the girls don't go out with the boys. In other areas the girls will go out during daylight and the boys at night, and then other areas, they just all go out together. In some areas, girls ride horses and the boys don't.

-Seventeen-
Oddbits
& Origins

"One Halloween, in the mid-1990s, I received a call from a mountain woman about her grandfather killing two peddlers back in Hopkins Gap in Rockingham County. He had given them a place to stay for the night and in the night he saw they were with his two daughters. So he shot them, and buried them out in the garden next to a revenuer he had killed the month before."[19]

I keep thinking, there's so much more out there, there just isn't enough time. I tell people that and they say, "How much do you enjoy doing this?" I say, "If I could do it twenty-four hours a day, I would do it. I'd just be back talking to people."

It's like the woman I told you about that I visited back in Pocahontas County. Originally I was supposed to talk to her older sister, who was twenty years older and she died before I could get back there. I got the eighty-one-year-old and talked to her.

In February of 2002 I traveled through a snowstorm across several mountains to visit the granddaughter of a Union bushwhacker in Arborvale, West Virginia. She had only one leg and felt compelled to show me how she could wiggle the other stump.

When people tell me, "You gotta talk to so and so." I try to do it, but a lot of times I don't.

I'd ask them a lot of standard question about things like witchcraft or foods. I always ask them about foods because they've changed a lot. Things that people ate that they enjoyed, like pigs feet jelly. I've talked to people who've had it and really liked it, and other people who just hate it. Or how to make souse. What's the difference between pon haus and scrapple? There is a difference. Things like that that people don't realize anymore.

Also, old farming techniques. I've actually talked to old men who said their job when they were young boys was after they would harrow the cornfield, then they would take another instrument and they would kind of checkerboard the field so that you had squares maybe two-and-a-half-feet on each side. Where those intersections were, they were to come along and poke a hole and drop three kernels of corn in it. That was their job.

It's funny that somebody still living had that job because by that time they had corn planters that were easier to use and certainly could do it a lot faster. In some areas they stayed by the old ways and even had old sayings.

A husband and wife would plant flaxseed together. He would cast a handful and hit the wife on the rump. He would cast the seed for the flax and she would say, "That high and higher too." It was a rhythm, every time he cast it. "That high and higher too." You had to do it just about daylight, you couldn't do it any later. You had to do it when it was still in that sunrise of morning.

There are so many things like that and I know there are so many more out there where I just haven't talked to that person yet who remembers that type of thing from their family.

Brocks Gap is where I first heard that instead of saying "thank you," you say, "I'll throw a rock into your garden sometime." Because if you say "thank you," it's bad luck. Say that to the wrong person who doesn't know what it means, "Well, hell with you. I just gave you a nice present, and you say you'll throw a rock in my garden. What's that mean?"

Apparently that was pretty prevalent back there so that you wouldn't bring bad luck down on anything. No, I remember what it was, if somebody gave you a plant, you would say it because if you didn't, it would die. And that would give the plant the strength to be able to survive under your care. "I'll throw a rock into your garden sometime."

That's the other thing that I've found too, in interviewing people, a lot of them have these stories but they also have things that they don't understand. Like the names of things. I was talking about the sheaves of wheat, the two at the top that would be fanned out over the shock of wheat to get moisture off of it as it sat out in the field. Most people called it a cap, but in some areas, in Highland and in Shenandoah, they called it a hudder. It might have been here in Augusta and Rockingham too, but I would say, "Why do you call it a hudder?" They'd say, "I don't know. We just always called it a hudder." So I get out my handy-dandy Pennsylvania German-English book and found out that hudder actually means a huddle, or a tangle. So that's what they were doing, they were jamming the ends together and spreading it all out in a tangle.

Nighttime pumpkin

There are other words like that too. My favorite one is when people were talking about harvest time and feeding the harvest crews that came in to help. This one woman said, "Oh, we'd make a huge fruit pie. It was just huge with great big flaps of dough that we'd put over the top of it after we got it filled up with fruit and berries. We called it a swanker pie." I asked, "Why swanker?" "I don't know, we just always called it a swanker pie." So again I go back to the handy-dandy Pennsylvania German-English dictionary and find "swanger," which means pregnant. Pregnant pie, this huge pie. When they talked about the pan they said it was like a dishpan it was so big that they built this pie in.

You know "schnickle fritz" is old Pennsylvania German, everybody uses that talking about cute kids. And what it really means is a wiggly child.

-Eighteen-
Superstitions

"The uplands of Virginia and West Virginia are beautiful and rich with the lore of the people who have come before. Stories of their wisdom, foolhardiness, joys and sorrows have been passed down through successive generations to us today. By knowing those things that made up the fabric of their lives, we can better understand why we are the way we are."[20]

Other things we'd talk about were superstitions. There's black cat superstitions and everybody knows those. But in different areas of the counties here in the Shenandoah Valley, if a black cat crosses your path from right to left, it's okay, but if he crosses it from left to right, then you're in trouble. You've got to turn around and go back.

I interviewed one woman who said, "My husband, if he'd start off for work and a black cat would cross in front of him he'd come home. He wouldn't go to work that day." (Laughter)

Over in New Hope here in Augusta County, this woman told me that if a black cat crossed in front of your car, you'd make an X with your finger on the windshield and then spit in your hat and throw it in the back seat. And hope nobody's back there, when it gets thrown back at you.

The other thing I found out that was really odd, is there's also a tradition in some areas here in the Valley of rabbits running in front of you being bad luck. Don't know where that comes from.

The other thing that I found out is about lucky rabbit's feet. They're not really lucky, most of them are just plain old rabbit's feet. They don't have any luck in them at all because to have a truly lucky rabbit's foot you have to have a foot from a rabbit that's killed in a graveyard on the night of a full moon by a cross-eyed man. That's the only way that they're lucky. Slim pickin's. But if you're cross-eyed you could go out and really make a fortune, "The only true lucky rabbits feet. From yours truly."

There are so many odd superstitions that it's really hard to remember them all. There's just so many of them. In Staunton, the black people used to think that if they heard a woodpecker outside of their house it meant that soon you'd be nailing nails into a coffin for somebody in the family. It's the only place I've ever found that, is in the black community.

You know "things that go bump in the night?" The thing that goes bump in the night is some kind of a message that somebody's going to die in the family.

There was an old woman who was a blood doctor, who lived over near McGaheysville, Jenny Life was her name, and they said that when she was older she was asleep up in her bed one night and she heard this "thump." Oh, it scared her to death and then another "thump," and then another "thump" and then another "thump" and then "thump, thump, thump, thump, thump, thump." They said it took them the longest time to get her settled down. What it was, a dog in the kitchen sleeping and probably dreaming about chasing rabbits or something and it was thumping its tail against the wall. It just drove her crazy. She thought, "This is it. This is it." All that thumping was going on.

Most groups have the tradition that if you bring a hoe into the house, or a shovel - a grave digging instrument - that's really bad luck to do something like that. The only way that you can break that hex is to turn around immediately and go out and make the sign of the cross with your foot on the doorframe, to keep bad things from happening.

Back in Greenbrier County, West Virginia, I interviewed a woman who said that they had that superstition too about bringing a shovel or a hoe into the house. This young man, I guess he was in his late teens, had a younger sister, who was five or six years old, she was playing out in the front yard near their car and he was out in the back hoeing in the garden. All of a sudden the little girl started screaming and she jumped up on to the hood of the car because a rattlesnake was right there coiled up next to her. The mother looked out of the front door and yelled to him in the back yard, "Hurry up! Bring the hoe, there's a rattlesnake out here that's got Sissy up on the hood of the car." He started to run through the house and she said, "NO! NO! NO! Go back out and come around the side. Don't come through the house with that hoe." (Laughter)

So if the snake had struck in that couple of seconds, the heck with it, we don't want bad luck in the house. Made him run out the door again. Crazy. She was the little girl, she said it happened. Eighty-year-old woman telling me that story.

CD: That's fascinating. I could listen to you all day and all night, John, but I won't put you to that.
JLH: You know what will happen is, you'll be down the road in half an hour and I'll think, why didn't I tell her that story?

-Nineteen-
Comedy Circuit

"Hopefully you have enjoyed this excursion through some of the word entertainments which were so much a part of the lives of the people who once lived in the mountains and valleys of the Virginias. Now that they are a part of you, please pass them on to some young person and you will have become an element of a wonderful folk tradition."[21]

I'd like to end on a funny story. I wonder if I have a funny story that I can just dig up and say all of a sudden.

One of my favorite ones, from Shenandoah County, is the young widow with children who had very little to help her family to survive. She had this one pig that she was going to butcher later on so they'd have some meat that winter. The pig got out and got over into a neighbor's bunch of hogs and pigs. She went over and asked for it, and the guy said, "No, show me that that's your pig."

"I'm telling you, that's my pig."

"I don't know that that's your pig, there's no mark on it or anything."

She left and she was really upset. She went to the local magistrate and told him the story. He said, "Okay, we'll ride out there and we'll talk to him." They rode out to the farm and got out of his car and walked over to the fence and the farmer came walking up. The magistrate says, "This woman tells me that that's her pig in there, and that's all she has to feed her family. I want to know, is that your pig or her pig?" The magistrate asked the woman, "Madame, can you point out your pig to me?"

She points to this one pig and says, "That's him right there."

Of course he's feeling really sorry for her and he says, "Is it marked or anything?"

She says, "No, but it's my pig, it's my pig."

He says, "Will you swear that that's your pig?"

She said, "Well, I hate to swear, but yes, damn it, that is my pig."

He laughed and said, "Okay, you take it on home then."

One more, one more. This one's really good. There's a woman who lived on Stony Creek, just outside of Edinburg and she loved to fish. She'd go out and get these night crawlers and she'd put them in a little bucket and put soil in with them. She talked one of her neighbors into going with her to fish one time. The first woman said, "Just be over here tomorrow morning. We'll get the bait out and get our rods and then we'll go out and do some fishing. You'll really enjoy this."

The neighbor woman showed up the next morning. The first woman was standing over her can of worms and she was going through it and she said, "I had a couple dozen night crawlers in here and I can't find a one of them."

Her neighbor said, "Don't you know that night crawlers are cannibalistic?"

The woman said, "Well, yes, damn it, but there ought to be at least one left."

It's so much fun. Twenty-four hours a day, I could just go on the folklore comedy circuit. Just stand up in front of people.

CD: You and Jim Britt [WSVA's co-host for John's Civil War program].

JLH: Jim is funny. And you go in there to the radio station any morning and there will be about ten or fifteen newspapers, he reads them all, that morning. So, he's got a lot of stuff going through his head but usually the newspapers don't have the folklore in them.

Did you see the *Daily News Record* [Harrisonburg, Virginia] today? I stole a page from it when I was in at the doctor's office this morning.

A woman who is an instructor over at JMU found a graveyard back in the George Washington National Forest, and she thinks it's a slave graveyard. They had pictures of the tombstones and they have symbols on them, there are no names. Just all these symbols, and she thinks that it might be the Ebu tribe in West Africa. She thinks that she can trace some of the symbols back to a couple of different tribes.

She thinks about twenty or thirty graves are there. There's only one or two that are marked with family names. That's gonna help her, to at least find out if it's a black cemetery.

The other ones with the symbols are really old. The symbols are really interesting looking.

CD: That's fascinating. I've heard the ones in Fulks Run aren't marked, the slave stones.
JLH: No, they wouldn't be. The only ones that I know of that are marked at all are just rough field stones, but these have all kinds of strange symbols.

She thinks that the reason it's so far back in is that they didn't want white people knowing about it. Her theory is that, she hasn't fully studied it yet, is that using those symbols, which to them, was supposedly a means to get to heaven or back to the mother country, that if white people saw them, they would think that it was witchcraft and destroy the graves or even the bodies that were in them. Of course it's all supposition.

The markers are so strange and so interesting that she might be on to something. If she is, it's the only known graveyard like this anywhere. There are a couple of good photographs in it too.

That's the other thing that I didn't talk about and I'll just finish up with that. Doing the interviews is one thing but also I try to be aware when an antique shop or an auction is selling family letters from a local area here in the Valley. I try to get them because a lot of times there will be things in those that are folkloric.

I bought a series of letters written from one teenage girl at

Grove Hill in Page County to a girl here in Augusta County at Parnassus. They just talk about all kinds of things; but they talked about superstitions sometimes too. If you take a thimbleful of salt and eat it and don't drink anything when you go to sleep that night, you'll dream of the man you're going to marry.

The Grove Hill girl is writing to this girl in Parnassus and she says, "I guess you've heard, my other younger sister has married, and they've left me to dance alone in the hog trough." What she meant was she was left behind to do all the chores because they got married and left the farm. So, "they've left me to dance alone in the hog trough," is how she put it.

You can find the material in all kinds of places. The oral histories in families are the best because the more you talk to the people about different things, the more they remember. Finding the old documents is important, too.

Okay. That's it!

CD: Thank you very much.
JLH: You're welcome.

John took a few minutes to show me his woodcarving bench. Tools hung on pegs, paint brushes filled jars, and cubicles covered the walls. John showed me his current work, which he later donated to the Skyline Literacy Auction. Mr. Mouse, dressed in a checkered coat and tie, strolls on the garden path, complete with spiral walking cane. At the Literacy auction on April 4, 2004, this five-by-five inch mouse carved out of a single block of linden wood, "The Path to the Garden Gate," sold for $6,200.

On my way out, I took a minute to telephone my husband. Watching me push the numbers on the telephone, John L. Heatwole, the man that could enchant listeners for hours with his phenomenal recall of folklore, marveled that I could remember my phone card number and pin without using a cheat sheet.

CD: On September 22 of 2005, John wrote this update about what he had been working on since our 2004 interview.

JLH: This year I have been writing interpretive signs for the Virginia Civil War Trails Initiative. So far I've written twenty-four in the Valley. I'm also working on an easement for the site where Lt. John R. Meigs was killed during the Civil War. I've done these before, but this one had special concerns because the property belongs to Old Order Mennonites. I was able to convince them that what happened at the site was a part of their history, too, because of the impact it had on their community when houses in a three-mile radius of the site were burned in retaliation for the lieutenant's death.

I'm still doing work with the Museum of the Shenandoah Valley on a limited basis. I'll do a talk there on Christmas Traditions in the Shenandoah Valley in December of this year. Sometime soon we'll begin filming and doing voice-overs for a video about Civil War sites in eastern Rockingham County and the Valley Pike. Last week I took the great grandson of Confederate General Isaac Trimble to the sites his ancestor knew in 1862.

I've given a number of talks this year, probably about thirty by the end of the year. I've been a speaker in four symposiums this year. I already have talks committed to as far ahead as 2007.

From 2003 to 2005, John worked closely with museum director, Jennifer Esler, and the Two Rivers multi-media production company, at the Museum of the Shenandoah Valley. John was key in getting in touch with people who had mutual interests, also using his contacts for the making of their introductory film—a gorgeous movie that captures the beauty and heart of the Shenandoah Valley. Throughout this beautiful museum in Winchester, Virginia, you can hear and see segments from dozens of interviews that John conducted.

Within the museum, several computers are set up, ready by simple instruction, to record a visitor's oral history of the Shenandoah Valley into their archive. John can be seen talking about oral history on these computers. When John conducted interviews, he

Courtesy Bruce Rossenwasser

**John, in his Bridgewater work-
shop, painting a drum in 1996.**

would start with a person's childhood, because those are the memories that last the longest, and then try to ask about all aspects of
their lives. "What were things you enjoyed? What did you fear?"

John says, "I think oral histories are the stories that were
important enough in a family to be passed down and told to their
children. And the children think they are important enough to be
told to their children and it keeps going over generations....

"I think it's important too because all those families with their
oral histories are part of a bigger patchwork quilt, if you will, of
that particular community and how everybody worked, interlock-
ing in their families."

John would often end his public talks with this advice: "Go
out and interview people."

Twenty

The Wizard of Wood & Words Dies

"Wouldn't it be interesting if I were to pass on and at the foot of my deathbed all of my carvings would assemble, not mere imaginings, but in the flesh, creatures and beings from the deep forest and secret mountain abodes."[22]

On November 22, 2006, a cold and icy morning with the kind of rain that seeps into your bones, John L. Heatwole died. He is sadly missed and will live on in our memories, through his work, and in the work he inspired in everyone around him.

When I was a child
I had dreams within dreams

John's childhood photos

A Brief Biography
John Lawrence Heatwole

Raised in Fairfax County, Virginia, John became interested in history, drawing, and carving at an early age. After a stint in the U.S. Marine Corps and work with the Library of Congress, John and his wife, Miriam, moved to Dayton, Virginia in the Shenandoah Valley.

During his years in the Valley, John served on numerous committees and boards of directors that related both to art and history. John served as co-chair of the Rockingham County Bicentennial Commission and was a long-time supporter of the Skyline Literacy Coalition, the Lincoln Society of Virginia, the Shenandoah Valley Folklore Society, the Harrisonburg-Rockingham Historical Society, Bridgewater College, and Massanutten Regional Libraries, to name a few.

A consultant for Time-Life Books and Public Broadcasting Service specials, John also hosted a folklore program on WREL in Lexington, Virginia. He was a well known and delightful radio personality with the longest running Civil War radio program in the country (co-hosted with Jim Britt and George Hansbrough) on WSVA in Harrisonburg, Virginia.

Author of **Shenandoah Voices - Folklore, Legends and Traditions of the Valley**; **The Virginia and West Virginia Mountain and Valley Folklife Series**; **A History of Chrisman's Boy Company** and **The Burning: Sheridan in the Shenandoah Valley**; all of John's work has received national acclaim.

In 1995, John was awarded the Shenandoah Valley Folklore Society Award, "for his work in preserving the history and oral traditions of the Shenandoah Valley." In 1998, he received the Shenandoah Valley Folk Arts Revival Society Award, "for his outstanding contributions to the cultural life of the Shenandoah Valley as an artist, folklorist, and oral historian." In 2002, he was pleasantly surprised to receive the Shenandoah University's President's Award for the Preservation of Community History. In 2006, John was honored with the Carrington Williams Preservation Award from the Shenandoah Valley Battlefields Foundation.

Howard Kittell, executive director of the Shenandoah Valley Battlefields Foundation, summarized John's historical work in the foundation's presentation of its award on October 31, 2006: "In 1997 John Heatwole was appointed to the Shenandoah Valley Battlefields National Historic District Commission by the Secretary of the Interior to represent Rockingham County. In this capacity he played a key role in crafting a plan to identify, preserve, interpret, and promote the Civil War battlefields and sites that constitute the National Historic District....

"During the three years of the commission's work, concluding in December 2000, and in subsequent years, Mr. Heatwole has been a passionate, active participant, a leader, and a supporter of the National Historic District and of the Shenandoah Valley Battlefields Foundation for which he served as a founding trustee.

"Mr. Heatwole has given unstintingly of his time, energy, and talent to collect and present the Shenandoah Valley's heritage and specifically its Civil War history. This was done through public lectures, educational programs, tours, publications, developing interpretive content and programs for museums, and on the radio. His efforts have stimulated an increased understanding of the importance of the Valley's Civil War battlefields and historic sites to local, state, and national elected officials, organizations, and individuals.... Mr. Heatwole has been an invaluable advisor, supporter, historian, advocate and friend of the Shenandoah Valley Battlefields Foundation...."

The Rockingham County, Virginia, Board of Supervisors passed a resolution honoring John, as quoted from *The Daily News Record,* Harrisonburg, Virginia, October 3, 2006: "Supervisor Bill Kyger read the resolution during a recent meeting of the board: 'Whereas, Mr. Heatwole's many accomplishments, known throughout the Commonwealth and the nation, have brought recognition to the Shenandoah Valley and to western Virginia... Now, therefore, be it resolved that the Rockingham County Board of Supervisors, acting on behalf of the citizens of Rockingham County, does hereby recognize and express sincere gratitude to John L. Heatwole for his contributions to enrichment of the quality of life in Rockingham County.'"

Awards continue to arrive posthumously. In March of 2007, the town of Bridgewater honored John's passing by reissuing the vehicle decal which John had drawn for them several years before. It is John's sketch of a grand old tree in Bridgewater with the words: John L. Heatwole, 1948-2006.

On March 1, 2007, John was awarded the Shenandoah Bowl from the Shenandoah Valley Travel Association for his significant contribution to the development of tourism in the Valley.

As his friend and fellow author, David Rodes, said of John, "It's as Edwin M. Stanton said of Abraham Lincoln, 'Now he belongs to the ages.'"

WVPT commissioned this oak tree drawing done by John in 1977. (Courtesy JMU Library Special Collections.)

Senate Joint Resolution Number 430
Celebrating the life of John L. Heatwole

Offered January 16, 2007
Agreed to by the Senate, February 1, 2007
Agreed to by the House of Delegates, February 9, 2007

Patrons — Obenshain and Hanger; Delegates: Landes, Lohr and Saxman

WHEREAS, John L. Heatwole of Swoope, a respected artisan and community benefactor, died on November 22, 2006; and

WHEREAS, John Heatwole shared his many talents as a sculptor, folklorist, historian, author, and lecturer with his fellow Virginians; and

WHEREAS, John Heatwole was born on March 24, 1948, and grew up in Washington, D.C., the son of Lillye Marie Preston and John L. Heatwole, Jr.; and

WHEREAS, John Heatwole served in the United States Marine Corps and was employed by the Library of Congress before moving to the Shenandoah Valley in 1974; and

WHEREAS, John Heatwole moved to the Shenandoah Valley convinced by his uncle, Paul Heatwole, to follow his passion of wood sculpting; he began working at Virginia Craftsmen, pursued a professional career as an artist, and within a few years opened his own shop in Bridgewater; and

WHEREAS, over the years, John Heatwole built a reputation as an imaginative artisan and he became well-known throughout the Valley; and

WHEREAS, an art director at Neiman Marcus department store in Washington, D.C., hired John Heatwole to produce figures for a 1979 Christmas window; the National Capitol Rotunda displayed his artwork in 1980; and the Harrisonburg-Rockingham Historical Society displayed more than 200 of his pieces at its museum in Dayton in 1982; and

WHEREAS, John Heatwole created a world of wizards, dwarfs, and magical figures, and he wrote in an article, "Fine Wood Working," that his creativity had sprung from a childhood filled with fear and anxiety; and

WHEREAS, also a celebrated storyteller, John Heatwole was passionate about Shenandoah Valley history, folklore, and superstition and wrote many books and lectured on the subjects at local events and on radio shows; and

WHEREAS, in 1995, John Heatwole wrote a book *Shenandoah Voices: Folklore, Legends, and Traditions of the Valley*, a collection of his interviews with colorful and fascinating people who grew up in the 19th & 20th centuries; and

WHEREAS, John Heatwole loved to explore the Shenandoah Valley's Civil War history, and in 1998 after years of painstaking research, he published *The Burning: Sheridan in the Shenandoah Valley*, describing the devastation civilians suffered as a result of General Sheridan's campaign in the fall of 1864; and

WHEREAS, John Heatwole served his community on the Rockingham County Bicentennial Commission, the Shenandoah Valley Battlefields National Historic District Commission, and the Shenandoah Valley Battlefields Foundation and was instrumental in preserving many historic and battlefield sites; and

WHEREAS, John Heatwole was honored with the Shenandoah University President's Award for Outstanding Service in Community History in 2002 and the Shenandoah Valley Battlefields Foundation's Carrington Williams Preservation Award in 2006; and

WHEREAS, John Heatwole will be greatly missed by his wife Miriam, his son David and daughter-in-law Dawn, his wonderful grandchildren, and numerous other loving family members and friends; now, therefore, be it

RESOLVED by the Senate, the House of Delegates concurring, That the General Assembly mourn the passing of a talented artisan and outstanding Virginian, John L. Heatwole; and, be it

RESOLVED FURTHER, That the Clerk of the Senate prepare a copy of this resolution for presentation to the family of John L. Heatwole as an expression of the General Assembly's respect for his memory.

Quotation citations

[1]Carol M. DeHart, John L. Heatwole (JLH), *The Word Gatherer*, Oral History Interview, Lot's Wife Publishing, Staunton, Virginia, 2007, 48.

[2]Interview with Miriam Heatwole by Carol DeHart, 2003.

[3]JLH, Personal Papers, 23 February 1980.

[4]Ibid., 15 October 1981.

[5]Ibid., 17 March 1980.

[6]Museum of the Shenandoah Valley, Shenandoah Exhibit, Winchester, Virginia, 6 March 2007.

[7]*The Washington Star*, Washington, D.C., 2 May 1980.

[8]JLH, Personal Papers, 8 October 1981.

[9]Ibid., 12 February 1980.

[10]JLH, Museum of the Shenandoah Valley, Winchester, Virginia, Oral History Video Archive, 6 March 2007.

[11]JLH, Personal Papers, 25 January 1981.

[12]JLH, *The Virginia and West Virginia Mountain and Valley Folklife Series - Superstitions*, Paul V. Heatwole Interview, Rockingham County, Virginia, 1997, 7.

[13]JLH, Personal Papers, 11 July 1981.

[14]JLH, *Shenandoah Voices: Folklore, Legends and Traditions of the Valley*, Rockbridge Publishing Company, Berryville, Virginia, 1995, 98.

[15]JLH, *Ibid.*, 103.

[16]JLH, *Valley Folklife Series - Witches and Witch Doctors*, 1997, 2.

[17]Ibid., *Magic Cures and Incantations*, Introduction, 1997, 1.

[18]Ibid., *Holidays and Pastimes*, 1998, 51.

[19]JLH, Oral History Interview, Follow-up answers, 22 September 2005.

[20]JLH, *Valley Folklife Series - Superstitions*, 1997, 20.

[21]Ibid., *Old Sayings, Proverbs, Riddles and Conundrums*, 2000, 46.

[22]JLH, Personal papers, on his thirty-third birthday, 24 March 1981.

Courtesy Pat Turner Ritchie

The placement of this historic signage marking the site where Union Lieutenant John Rogers Meigs fell was a dream of John's that was fulfilled by his friends and colleagues after his death.

Index

John was a cross between an historian and a folklorist. He was able to connect many of the stories he recorded with historical documents such as this Staunton newspaper advertisement from 1866 that mentions many of the herbs that he learned about in his travels and encounters.

Acknowledgments

To all of you wonderful people who have been so very gener-
ous and kind, your assistance in publishing this book is
greatly appreciated:

John's immediate family, Miriam and David Heatwole,
and Stephanie Price;

Jennifer Esler, director of the beautiful Museum of the
Shenandoah Valley in Winchester, and Julie B. Armel, the
museum's public relations and marketing coordinator, as well
as the rest of the welcoming museum and bookstore staff;

Howard Kittell, Executive Director of the Shenandoah
Valley Battlefields Foundation in New Market, Virginia, as
well as other members of the Foundation's Interpretation
and Education Committee;

Dr. Phillip Stone, President of Bridgewater College, in
Bridgewater, Virginia;

Tracy Harter, head librarian, James Madison University Library, Special Collections;

Greg Weber, proof reading law professor/mediator;

A few of John's friends: Two-Gun Terry, Jim and Julie
Swope, David Rodes, Ken and Betty Schuler, Allen Litten,
Patricia Turner Ritchie, Bruce Rossenwasser, and especially,
Nancy Sorrells and Lot's Wife Publishing;

Rick and Jo Bowman, owners of Crafty Hands at the
Dayton Farmer's Market in Rockingham County, Virginia.

Thank you all.

Carol Maureen DeHart
October, 2007